still more
HOT
Illustrations
FOR
Youth Talks

100 *MORE* attention-getting stories, parables, & anecdotes

still more

HOT Illustrations FOR Youth Talks

100 MORE attention-getting stories, parables, & anecdotes

Wayne Rice

Youth Specialties

ZondervanPublishingHouse

Grand Rapids, Michigan
A Division of HarperCollinsPublishers

Still More Hot Illustrations for Youth Talks: 100 More Attention-Getting Stories, Parables, & Anecdotes

Copyright © 1999 by Youth Specialties, Inc.

Youth Specialties Books, 300 S. Pierce St., El Cajon, CA 92021, are published by Zondervan Publishing House, 5300 Patterson Ave. S.E., Grand Rapids, MI 49530.

Library of Congress Cataloging-in-Publication Data

Still more hot illustrations for youth talks : 100 more attention-getting stories, parables, & anecdotes / [compiled by] Wayne Rice :
   with contributions from many of America's top youth communicators, Stan Beard . . . [et al.].
        p.   cm.
       Includes index.
       ISBN 0-310-22464-0
       1. Homiletical illustrations. 2. Preaching to youth. I. Rice, Wayne.
   BV4225.S75   1999
   252'.08—dc21
                                              98-51646
                                               CIP

The author and publisher acknowledge that some of the stories in this volume are of unknown origin, having been circulated orally or electronically, and without bylines or other identifying information. We've made every effort to track down the source of each story in this book. We apologize for any omissions.

We're grateful to the writers, publishers, and contributors of *all* the stories in this volume—and especially for the use of the following stories:

All Is Forgiven: from "The Capital of the World" from *The Short Stories,* Ernest Hemingway (Scribner, 1995).

Bad Math, Good Play: from *Following Jesus without Embarrassing God,* Tony Campolo (Word Publishers, 1997). Used by permission. All rights reserved.

Big Rocks: from *First Things First,* Steven Covey (Simon & Schuster, 1994).

Come Home: excerpted from *No Wonder They Call Him the Savior,* by Max Lucado, Multnomah Publishers, Inc., ©1986 by Multnomah Publishers. Reprinted by permission.

The Day of the Rabbit: excerpted from "The Fall" from *A Severe Mercy* by Sheldon Vanauken. ©1977, 1980 by Sheldon Vanauken. Reprinted by permission of HarperCollins Publishers, Inc.

The Farmer's Three Wishes: excerpted from John Claypool, *Stories Jesus Still Tells* (McCracken Press, 1993).

The Golden Fish: from the Associated Press story "Family Lives Out Golden Balkan Fairy Tale," from *The San Diego Union-Tribune* (June 7, 1998).

How to Train an Elephant: from *Generation Next,* George Barna (Regal, 1995).

The Mirror: from *It Was on Fire When I Lay Down on It* by Robert Fulghum. ©1988, 1989 by Robert Fulghum. Adapted by permission of Villard Books, a division of Random House, Inc.

The Street Bum: from *Following Jesus without Embarrassing God,* Tony Campolo (Word Publishers, 1997). Used by permission. All rights reserved.

Take Me to Your Leader: adapted from *The Friendly Story Caravan,* Anna Pettit Broomell (Lippincott, 1962, out of print).

Too Polite: from *The Christian's Secret to a Happy Life,* Hannah Whitall Smith, as quoted in *Safe within Your Love: A 40-day Journey in the Company of Hannah Whitall Smith,* David Hazard (Bethany House, 1992).

Edited by Cheri McLaughlin
Cover and interior design by PAZ Design Group
Illustrations by Joyce Revoir

Printed in the United States of America

99 00 01 02 03 04 05 / / 15 14 13 12 11 10 9 8 7 6 5 4 3 2 1

Contents

Alphabetical List of Illustrations

95850

Quick Illustration Locator
By Topic

Still More **Hot Illustrations for Youth Talks**

Quick Illustration Locator
By Scripture

Introduction
Choosing and Using Illustrations

A wealthy businessman from New York purchased 250 acres of prime beachfront property in Maui and built on it the finest resort hotel in the islands. It was a truly magnificent property, with more than 2,000 elegant suites, 14 swimming pools with giant water slides, a roller coaster, nine restaurants, a shopping complex, a health club, a championship golf course, and every possible amenity you can imagine. Called Heavenly Kingdom, it was a theme park, hotel, and shopping mall all rolled into one.

Now, because the businessman spent most of his time in New York, he hired a local management firm, CP&P Enterprises, to manage the hotel in exchange for a percentage of the profits. Needless to say, the resort was a huge success. Tourists from all over the world came to visit Heavenly Kingdom. The hotel was booked years in advance, and the money was rolling in. Clearly, the businessman was going to make a healthy return on his investment.

But after two years of operation, the businessman still hadn't made any money from his venture. CP&P reported huge losses instead of profits. The puzzled businessman sent three of his associates from New York to find out what was going on and to collect what was due him. When they arrived, however, they were not treated kindly. One of the men was beaten and robbed in the hotel parking lot. The second was roughed up and thrown out of the hotel by security guards. The third was found dead several days later, his body washed up on the beach. Local authorities were unable to determine if the man's death was the result of foul play.

The shocked businessman desperately tried to contact CP&P but got no response whatsoever. So he sent a second group of men to Maui to finish the job and to bring back what was rightfully his. But when they arrived, they suffered a worse fate than the others. On the way to the hotel, the limo they were riding in was run off the road, and it careened over a steep embankment, killing everyone on board.

The businessman finally decided to go to Maui himself.

"Wait," said his son. "Let me go instead. I'm closer to their age, and I can speak their language. There's a good chance that they'll listen to me if I go alone in peace." Reluctantly, the businessman agreed to let his son make the dangerous trip to Maui.

When the bosses at CP&P found out that the owner's son was on his way, they started scheming. "Put a contract out on him," they said. "Once he's gone, the old man will finally leave us alone, and we'll have the resort all to ourselves!" A few days later, authorities found the son's body stuffed in a garbage bag at the bottom of a dumpster.

As you can imagine, the businessman was grief-stricken—but he was also enraged. He unleashed his wrath on the scoundrels running CP&P Enterprises, marshaling every resource at his disposal to round them up and prosecute them to the fullest extent of the law. Juries found each defendant guilty of charges from racketeering to murder one. The defendants all served life sentences without parole.

The businessman set about restoring trustworthy management to Heavenly Kingdom, and the resort prospered under the new administrators. Miraculously, the businessman's son survived his ordeal and eventually took over all his father's businesses.

Everybody loves a happy ending. Unless, of course, the happy ending has you being thrown in the slammer. When Jesus originally told this story ("The Parable of the Tenants" in Matthew 21:33-44), the chief priests and Pharisees didn't like the ending at all. According to Scripture, after hearing this parable they immediately began plotting Jesus' arrest. Why? It didn't take a rocket scientist to figure out who CP&P Enterprises really was (Matthew 21:45). Jesus never had to mention their names. All he had to do was tell a story.

Jesus appreciated the power of a good anecdote. In fact, Scripture records that Jesus *never* spoke without using a parable (Matthew 13:34). He consistently sprinkled his teaching with stories and real-life situations to drive home his points. He drew his illustrations from everyday life in the

Middle East, describing farmers and families, sheep and goats, barns and wheat fields—and people were amazed at his teaching (Matthew 7:28).

Amazing is not how most teenagers describe church speakers and teachers. *Borrring* seems more like it. A few speakers, however, know how to capture the attention of kids and can communicate well with them. Invariably these speakers effectively use stories in their talks.

This book, like the first two in the *Hot Illustrations* series, is a selected compilation of 100 stories that speakers have used effectively in youth talks. I have used many of them myself. All of them work with kids if they are chosen with care and communicated with conviction and purpose.

Adults enjoy them as well. In fact, I think we're wrong to assume that adults prefer dull and boring abstractions to interesting and colorful illustrations. I find that the best way to communicate with adults is to speak to them as if they're all about 14 years old. (That assumes, of course, that you don't speak to 14-year-olds like they're children.)

This is not an exhaustive collection of illustrations. Those books which claim to be exhaustive are often too large and difficult to use. I have one book on my shelf boasting of nearly 8,000 anecdotes. But to be honest, it's hard for me to find one good illustration in that book when I need it. My goal for the *Hot Illustrations* series has been to offer you quality illustrations rather than *quantity.*

Since selecting and using stories is a subjective and personal exercise, what works for you may not work for me (and vice versa). Nevertheless, this book offers you a good sampling of illustrations I can recommend without reservation. Much of my confidence has to do with the quality people who contributed to this book (whose names you'll find on page 185), and I thank all of them for sharing their material with us. I know the value of good anecdotes—they're hard to come by. Many speakers prefer keeping their stories to themselves. We who do regular public speaking are indebted to all those who contributed to this book.

Choose the concrete, the interesting, and the unpredictable.

An effective story uses concrete images—familiar to the hearer and

drawn from everyday life. Even the most illiterate, uneducated peasant could identify with the situations, objects, and people Jesus described in his parables. One reason the old hymn "Amazing Grace" has remained popular over the years is because of its familiar, concrete language.

Amazing grace, how sweet the sound, that saved a wretch like me. I once was lost, but now I'm found, was blind but now I see.

Contrast those stirring words with the following version:

Unexpected lenience, in the form of a mellifluous tonality, preserved an organism of questionable value commonly associated with the author of this composition. Said ego was one time misplaced, but the situation has been altered, and currently, there is no doubt as to its location. In addition, said ego formerly was incapacitated by a malfunction of the visual sense, but at this moment has recovered the associated ability.

If you think this rendition is hard to understand, try *singing* it.

Along with using concrete images, a good illustration is interesting. A story needs a plot that engages the listener all the way to its conclusion. Take, for example, the parables Jesus told. People caught up in his stories lowered their defenses, allowing Jesus to drop a truth bomb on them.

Finally, and perhaps most importantly, an effective illustration uses surprise. The unpredictable climax is what makes a joke funny, a movie suspenseful, and an anecdote powerful. Surprise helps drive a message home. Surprises are remembered. More than once Jesus' illustrations captivated listeners who were comfortable in their certainty that the point was meant for some other group of people. Then, watch out! The ending pointed the finger at themselves.

The Old Testament prophet Nathan used the element of surprise to change King David's opinion about his adultery and murder. When David heard Nathan's story of the rich man with many sheep who confiscated from the poor man his one pet lamb, David became incensed (2 Samuel 12). He angrily demanded that the evil rich man be brought to justice.

What a surprise when Nathan enlightened David that he had just pronounced judgment on himself.

Start by choosing the point of your talk, not by finding a riveting illustration.

Illustrations are not the points you're attempting to communicate. Don't build your talk around a story you're eager to use. Decide the truth you want to make known, and then find or create an illustration that will breathe life into it.

A young boy received a bow and arrow from his father and immediately went outside to try it out. Checking on his boy a few minutes later, the father was amazed to see that the boy had hit the bull's-eye in several targets crudely drawn on the side of a fence. Impressed by his son's achievement, he said to his son, "I didn't realize you were such a good shot!"

"Oh it was easy," the boy replied. "I shot the arrows first, then drew the targets around them."

Creating a talk around an illustration is like drawing targets around your arrows. First draw your target—decide what truth you desire to communicate. Once you know where your arrow needs to end up, speed it on its way with a fitting anecdote.

To help you match your talk with an anecdote, consult the topical listing on page 6. Also, each story in this book is followed with a suggestion or two about "where to take it from here." However, since every story has an unlimited number of applications, my recommendations are only the most obvious applications.

When your point is obvious, don't illustrate it.

Suppose I stood up in front of a group and said, "God is good." The truth of that claim may not be clear to some people. I probably need to illustrate it with a story, example, or analogy that describes what I mean. If,

however, your group was meeting in a room registering 40 degrees on the thermostat and I said, "This room is cold," then an illustration would belabor the point. My audience doesn't need to be enlightened by a story about someone freezing to death.

Limit the number of illustrations you use in one talk.

One good anecdote per point is usually plenty. Listeners are influenced for a longer time by a single illustration than by a point that's cluttered with several stories. If your friend tells you one joke, for example, you'll probably tell it yourself to a few other friends. But if your friend tells you *two* jokes, by the time you're through laughing at the second joke, you'll likely have already forgotten the first one.

A seminar speaker I heard recently must have used 20 or more stories one evening. The audience laughed throughout the session. Yet in spite of the quality illustrations, I found it difficult afterward to remember any of them, not to mention the *point* of any of them. Make your point and illustrate it well, then move on to another point—or just stop. Piling illustration upon illustration is like continuing to hammer a nail once the nail is in all the way—after that, all the hammer does is batter the wood.

Leave your audience room to think for themselves.

An audience can feel put off if you pre chew a point and attempt to serve it up to them with an explicit application. At times it's appropriate to make sure that the audience gets the point quickly by explaining it in detail. Jesus explained to his close disciples the meaning of the symbols in the parable of the sower, for instance. But most of the time, Jesus simply told a story and then allowed his audience to think about it for a while and to discuss its meaning among themselves. Sometimes the listeners came to different conclusions. That's okay.

When Jesus' disciples asked him why he used parables, he explained that parables allowed those with an open heart to hear what God wanted them to hear (Matthew 13:10-17). But those with "hardened hearts" were kept in the dark. Jesus stimulated his disciples to learn by allowing them to ponder on their own the meaning of his parables (Matthew 13:36). And of course, we are also the beneficiaries of this strategy of the Master Teacher.

Use illustrations to recapture the audience's attention.

I'm always amazed at how an audience can be dozing off, doodling on program covers, whispering to each other—and then the speaker starts telling a story. On cue, everyone's head raises and every eye turns to the speaker. Unfortunately, what usually follows that magic moment of undivided attention is the end of the story—at which time everyone goes back to what they were doing.

A good speaker avoids this disheartening experience by making his application as poignant (without using the word *poignant)* and interesting as the story itself. That's why I warned you earlier to build your talk first and then select your illustration. A properly chosen story merely whets the appetite of the audience—they'll stay tuned to discover what your point is.

Change the pace in your talk by using illustrations.

When you're ready to shift gears in a talk, you may select an illustration for no other reason than to set up the audience for the point you're moving toward. In other words, the illustration may not communicate the truth you have in mind, but its humor serves as an ice breaker, its suprise opens the door on a new topic, its sentiment softens a challenge so the listeners stay with you to your conclusion.

Jokes, of course, are useful pace changers. I've used "The King of the Universe" (page 145) many times with kids to set up a talk on self-image or on the attributes of God. I present it as a joke, and then, like with any other anecdote, I tie it in to my main purpose. An effective speaker makes illustrations do meaningful work.

Although illustrations *may* be used merely to hold a group's attention or to get laughs, if those are their only purposes, the audience will become frustrated and bored. Like the boy who cried, "Wolf!" when there was no wolf, the audience eventually tires of a speaker who has no content to his message.

I attended a function a few years ago which featured a well-known speaker, popular on the banquet circuit. He used dozens of jokes, stories, and illustrations—some of them very entertaining. But his disjointed talk never went anywhere. He had no point to make—or if he did, he never developed it in such a way that the audience could remember what it was. In spite of the continuing laughter that greeted the speaker's funny stories, after an hour I could tell that the audience had had enough. They wanted to go home. Speakers who are light on content and heavy on entertainment are often insecure people whose primary concern is not to communicate a message, but to make the audience like them. That's okay if you're a standup comic, but not if you're entrusted with the life-changing message of the gospel.

Choose illustrations you can tell with authenticity.

Some of the illustrations in this book need to be communicated with a dramatic flair or with casual humor. If telling a joke makes you tense or if your most dramatic moment was placing an exclamation mark in a letter to your church's director of Christian education, you may want to avoid telling stories requiring flair for humor—or at least save it for when you loosen up.

As you consider whether to use a particular illustration, ask yourself, "How comfortable will I feel using this one? Is this me?" I remember trying to do Bill Cosby impressions when I was younger—and making a complete fool of myself. I couldn't understand why it was so funny when Bill Cosby did it and a bomb when I used the same routines. I know now. It's because I'm stuck with being me, not Bill Cosby. Since discovering that truth, when I speak I limit my illustrations to those which I can communicate with credibility and conviction.

Once you select an story from among the many in this book that fit your style, rehearse until you can present it convincingly. Memorize it if necessary. There's nothing worse than launching into an illustration only to realize halfway through it I forgot the part that made the illustration work. It's hard to go back and salvage the point. Believe me. I know.

Some of the stories in this book are meant to be read to the audience, such as "The Test" on page 166. If you're in the early experimental stages of using illustrations, try these first. Just photocopy the appropriate page and tuck it into your Bible or lesson book. Don't read directly from this book.

Choose illustrations with your audience in mind.

Not all illustrations are appropriate for every audience. The anecdotes in this book were selected primarily because they are, generally speaking, effective with adolescents. That doesn't mean they deal only with adolescent concerns. It just means that adolescents are the group that will best relate to the stories and get the point if you communicate it well.

Most of the illustrations in this book are stories, as opposed to quotes or statistics. That's because adolescents love stories—particularly stories that teach a lesson. Teenagers enjoy the often new experience of making connections between concrete illustrations and abstract ideas.

Make a distinction between true stories and stories that communicate truth.

Most anecdotes are not entirely true to begin with—even those that happen to you. I'll tell you right up front that none of the illustrations in this book are true. Some of them are based on historical events, such as "The Coach" and "Bad Math, Good Play," but they are presented here as illustrations, not history. In the telling and retelling of these anecdotes, they've been altered and embellished to make them effective illustrations. At best, they're only partially true. Tony Campolo likes to wink and

say about some of his anecdotes: "Well, if it didn't happen that way, it should have."

Illustrations, including the ones offered in this book and most of the stories that Jesus told, are nothing more than stories or parables that communicate truth. Parables are, by definition, fictional. Jesus made up his parables. There never was an actual Prodigal Son, as far as we know. Jesus invented the story to illustrate a point and did it so well that it has become one of the most beloved stories of all time.

Personalize your illustrations.

Enliven anecdotes by adding color to them, changing the details, renaming the characters, and generally tailor-making them to your audience—especially when you're telling a story from the Bible. Kids listen better when they can relate the story to familiar people, places, and events. Teenagers better identify with the prodigal son, for instance, if he's presented as a high school dropout who left home with his pockets full of cash.

Although personalizing illustrations enhances their effectiveness, don't lie to make yourself look important, look good, or even look bad. Be honest with your audience; you'll not only be more effective, but you'll have nothing that can come back later to haunt you.

With some stories personalizing is a breeze. If you're telling "The Flat Tire," for instance (page 63), you might say, "When I was in college, I hated final exams. No matter how hard I prepared, the test would be about stuff I never bothered to study. I guess I'm not alone, though. I read recently about a couple of guys who really blew it at exam time. Here's what happened..." You've personalized the story without telling a lie.

What you *don't* want to say is, "When I was in college, my friend and I were taking organic chemistry..." unless, of course, you actually *did* take organic chemistry and did what the guys in the story did. A famous Christian youth speaker recently lost his entire ministry when it was discovered that much of what he had claimed to be true over the years was

actually false. No talk is important enough to lie for. Anything short of the truth is unethical and has no place in the ministry of the church.

Credit the source of the illustrations you use.

Telling someone else's story as if it happened to you or as if you thought of it is a form of plagiarism, in most cases. I know several speakers who can hardly use their own talks anymore because other people have "stolen" their illustrations and examples and made them their own. Tony Campolo laughs about the time he was about to deliver his famous "It's Friday, but Sunday's Comin'" message to a church. The pastor urged him not to "because my congregation thinks that story happened to me."

The best way to use an illustration associated with someone else is to simply credit the source. If that pastor had only said, "Tony Campolo tells a wonderful story about the time he…" Of course, that disclaimer might lessen the effectiveness of the illustration—in which case it may not be the best one to use at all.

This book contains few illustrations personal to an individual speaker. That kind is difficult to transfer to yourself or to tell in the third person. I've compiled only those anecdotes that anyone can use.

Good illustrations also show up in your own life experiences and in the life experiences of others you know. Powerful illustrations can be derived from television, the movies, books, magazines, newspapers. Keep your eyes and ears open, and file your discoveries for future use.

In short, your goal is the accurate communication of the truth, so that what you say matches what your students hear, understand, and apply. I trust this book will help you achieve that goal next time you stand in front of an adolescent audience.

Earthly Treasures

Knowing he would die soon, a rich man had all his assets converted into gold bars, put them in a big bag on his bed, draped his body over the bag of gold, and breathed his last. When he woke up, he was at the gate of Heaven.

Saint Peter met him at the gate and with a concerned look on his face said, "Well, I see you actually managed to get here with something from earth! But unfortunately, you can't bring that in."

"Oh please, sir," said the man. "I must have it. It means everything to me."

"Sorry, my friend," said Saint Peter. "If you want to keep that bag, then I'm afraid you'll have to go to, you know, the other place. You don't want to go there, believe me."

"Well, I won't part with this bag."

"Have it your way," returned Peter. "But before you go, would you mind if I looked in the bag to see what it is that you're willing to trade eternal life for?"

"Sure," said the man. "You'll see. I could never part with this."

Saint Peter looked in the bag and with a puzzled look on his face said to the man, "You're willing to go to hell for...pavement?"

Where to take it from here...

What's coming between you and God? Your money? Your possessions? Your status? Your friends? Your fun? You may be sure that none of it can compare with what God has prepared for you (1 Corinthians 2:9). "What good will it be for a man if he gains the whole world, yet forfeits his soul?" (Matthew 16:26).

ONLY IN THE MOVIES

Here's a list of things you can learn from watching too many movies or TV shows:

- Most dogs are immortal.
- All grocery shopping bags contain at least one stick of French Bread.
- It's easy for anyone to land a plane, providing there's someone in the control tower to talk you down.
- Once applied, lipstick will never rub off—even while scuba diving.
- The ventilation system of any building is the perfect hiding place. No one will ever think of looking for you in there, and you can travel to any other part of the building you want without difficulty.
- If you need to reload your gun, you will always have more ammunition—even if you haven't been carrying any before now.
- You're very likely to survive any battle in any war, unless you make the mistake of showing someone a picture of your sweetheart back home.
- Should you wish to pass yourself off as a German officer, it will not be necessary to speak the language. A German accent will do.
- If your town is threatened by an imminent natural disaster or killer beast, the mayor's first concern will be the tourist trade or his forthcoming art exhibition.
- The Eiffel Tower can be seen from any window in Paris.
- A man will show no pain while taking the most ferocious beating, but will wince when a woman tries to clean his wounds.
- If a large pane of glass is visible, someone will be thrown through it before long.
- When paying for a taxi, don't look at your wallet as you take out a bill—just grab one at random and hand it over. It will always be the exact fare.
- Interbreeding is genetically possible with any creature from elsewhere in the universe.

- If staying in a haunted house, women should investigate any strange noises in their most revealing garments.
- Word processors never display a cursor on screen but will always say: Enter Password Now.
- Cars that crash will almost always burst into flames.
- A single match will be sufficient to light up a room the size of a football stadium.
- Medieval peasants had perfect teeth.
- It is not necessary to say hello or goodbye when beginning or ending phone conversations.
- Even when driving down a perfectly straight road it is necessary to turn the steering wheel vigorously from left to right every few moments.
- All bombs are fitted with electronic timing devices with large red readouts so you know exactly when they're going to go off.
- It's always possible to park directly outside the building you're visiting.
- A detective can only solve a case once he has been suspended from duty.
- If you decide to start dancing in the street, everyone you bump into will know all the steps.
- Most laptop computers are powerful enough to override the communication systems of any invading alien civilization.
- It does not matter if you are heavily outnumbered in a fight involving martial arts—your enemies will wait patiently to attack you one by one by dancing around in a threatening manner until you have knocked out the ones before them.
- When a person is knocked unconscious by a blow to the head, they will never suffer a concussion or brain damage.
- No one involved in a car chase, hijacking, explosion, volcanic eruption, or alien invasion will ever go into shock.

(continued)

- Police departments give their officers personality tests to make sure they are deliberately assigned a partner who is their total opposite.
- When they're alone, all foreigners prefer to speak English to each other.
- You can always find a chain saw when you need one.
- Any lock can be picked in seconds by a credit card or a paper clip—unless it's the door to a burning building with a child trapped inside.
- Television news bulletins usually contain a story that affects you personally at that precise moment.
- People rarely use the bathroom, and if they do, they're usually dead within minutes.
- You can always rely on your car keys already being in the ignition when you get in the car, but if it's an emergency you can't find the keys anywhere.
- No one locks doors, and if they do, chances are there's a hatchet about to come through it.

Where to take it from here...

TV and the movies rarely depict real life accurately. The electronic media's primary purpose is to entertain rather than to teach. For that one reason alone, never take TV shows or movies seriously—especially in their portrayal of Christian values and beliefs. Even though millions of people in America profess faith in Christ, Christians are nonexistent in the movies. And even though the vast majority of people in our country believe that sex should be reserved for marriage, few married people in the movies ever have sex—only unmarried people do.

When you watch TV or go to the movies, keep in mind that what you just saw probably could never (and should never) happen in real life. Don't let yourself be influenced by a lie.

The Flight of Larry Walters

A true story.

A few years ago 33-year-old truck driver Larry Walters made national news. Larry had a habit of spending his weekends in his Los Angeles backyard, just south of L.A. International Airport, drinking...Pepsi...and eating peanut butter sandwiches. He would sit in his favorite lawn chair staring at the houses around him in the subdivision where he lived. Not a real exciting life.

One day abject boredom prompted Larry Walters to buy some balloons and a tank of helium. He figured on tying the balloons to his lawn chair, filling them with helium, and floating up for an aerial view of the neighborhood. He judged he'd get no higher than 100 feet, but just in case, he got out his BB gun and loaded it. He planned to regulate his altitude by shooting out a couple of balloons. I'm not sure how many six-packs of...Pepsi...he had consumed when he came to that idea, but he decided it was worth a try.

So Larry Walters of Los Angeles went out and bought 45 big weather balloons, a huge tank of helium, and some rope. First he secured his lawn chair to the ground, then he filled the balloons with helium. One by one he tied them to his lawn chair. Before liftoff he went in the house and got another six-pack of...Pepsi, a couple of peanut butter and jelly sandwiches, and his BB gun. Then he went out and sat in his lawn chair. He had instructed his neighbors to cut the ropes securing the chair when he was ready. "Let's go!" he yelled, and the ropes were cut.

But he didn't go 100 feet. He went up 11,000 feet! Shot straight up in the air! And the BB gun? It was useless since he was using both hands to hang on to the chair for dear life.

He zoomed straight up into the landing pattern at L.A. Airport. The pilot of an approaching Continental DC 10 reported that he had just passed a man in a lawn chair, and the control tower told him to report in immediately upon landing. They thought the *pilot* may have been drinking a little too much...Pepsi. Can you imagine being a passenger in that plane? "Look, mom, out the window! There's a man in a lawn chair!"

Eventually they sent up helicopters to rescue Larry Walters. They closed the airport and diverted all landings and takeoffs at LAX while they played tag with this fellow in his lawn chair at 11,000 feet. When they finally got him down, he was surrounded by TV crews, the police, fire and rescue squads, and plenty of curious people. It was a major event.

"Were you scared?" asked one of the TV reporters, thrusting a mic in his face.

"No, not really" said Larry.

"Are you going to do it again?" asked another reporter.

"No," said Larry.

"What in the world made you do it the first time?"

Larry Walters thought about it for a moment and said, "Well, you can't just sit there."

Where to take it from here...

Larry Walters is right. You can't just sit there. God has something exciting for you to do. Don't be content to just sit there wasting time, doing nothing. Don't go through life watching from the sidelines while everyone else plays the game. God wants you to be a participant! (John 10:10).

Room in the Lifeboats

Catering to the rich and famous, this luxury liner was advertised as unsinkable. On *Titanic's* fateful night, passengers who somehow still believed the advertisement refused to get in the lifeboats, even though they were told the ship was going down. They held to their belief in the advertisement that the ship was unsinkable—and were actually offended by officers who told them to climb into a cramped lifeboat when they had paid enormous sums for luxurious accommodations.

Other passengers were unable to enter a lifeboat because of the selfish privileged who felt no concern for anyone but themselves. The first-class passengers feared that added weight in the lifeboats would jeopardize their chance for survival. As a result, many of the ship's lifeboats, which were made to hold up to 60 people, left the ship with only 15 people aboard.

Although there were enough lifeboats to save hundreds more, people either refused to use them or they were left stranded on the sinking liner.

Where to take it from here...

The death and resurrection of Jesus Christ provided the lifeboat we all must climb aboard. To miss that lifeboat is to perish. Many people either continue to believe that the world can offer them happiness or salvation through their own efforts, or they are left stranded because Christians have been too selfish to reach out to them. There is more than enough room at the Cross for those who are perishing.

The Smallest Piece

A fourteenth-century Italian stained-glass artist was summoned to design and create a huge portrait for the window of a cathedral in Chartres, France, a place well known for its stained-glass work. He laid all of the pieces he was going to use out on the floor of the cathedral. They were beautiful to behold; most of them were large and colorful. Some of the colors from that time cannot even be reproduced today. Among these awesome pieces of glass was a small, clear piece about as big as your fingernail. As the stained-glass portrait was assembled, that little piece remained on the floor. Only the big colorful pieces of glass were used.

On the day of the window's completion, the tiny piece of clear glass was still lying on the ground. The entire city gathered to witness the unveiling of the brilliant and beautiful stained-glass portrait. The artist stood in front of the crowd, made his speech, and dramatically pulled down the cloth cover. The crowd gasped at the beauty of the colorful window glowing in the sunlight.

After a few seconds, however, the crowd grew silent. They sensed that something was missing, that the portrait was unfinished. The great artist then walked over to where the little clear piece of glass lay, picked it up, and placed it in the portrait, right in the center of Jesus' eye. As the sun hit that little piece, it gave off a dazzling sparkle.

The magnificent stained glass window still draws visitors. The first thing they see is that sparkle in Jesus' eye.

Where to take it from here...

Do you ever feel like that little piece of clear glass? Left out. Untalented. A disappointment. You doubt you can ever do anything for God. Let the story of that last little piece remind you that God thinks of you as the apple of his eye (Psalm 17:8). No matter that in your eyes you don't measure up to others; you are an important part of the body of Christ. (1 Corinthians 12).

Still More Hot Illustrations for Youth Talks

Bad Math, Good Play

Oklahoma State University's 1996 season quarterback, President Lyndon Johnson's nephew Randy Johnson, proved to be a mediocre quarterback for a mediocre team. But mediocre or not, quarterbacks and teams and Oklahoma State could be lifted to legendary greatness if they beat their arch rival, the University of Oklahoma, in the season-ending game.

In that final game of 1996, Oklahoma was behind by six points. Little hope remained that they would score with almost 80 yards between them and their goal line, only minutes left on the clock, and a steady downpour of rain. But their mud-covered suits didn't look half as pitiful as the battered, despairing faces of the State players.

As a gesture of goodwill, the Oklahoma State coach put in all the seniors for the last play of the game and told Randy to call whatever play he wanted. The team huddled, and to the surprise of his teammates, Randy called play 13—a trick play they'd never used, for the good reason that it had never worked in practice.

Well, the impossible happened! Play 13 worked! Oklahoma State scored! Randy Johnson's team won the game by one point! The fans went wild! As they carried Randy, the hero of the game, off the field, his coach called out to him, "Why in the world did you ever call play 13?"

"Well, we were in the huddle," Randy answered, "and I looked over and saw old Harry with tears running down his cheeks. It was his last college game and we were losing. And I saw that big 8 on his chest. Then I looked over and saw Ralph. And tears were running down his cheeks, too. And I saw that big 7 on his jersey. So in honor of those two heart-broken seniors, I added eight and seven together and called play 13!"

"But Randy," the coach shouted back. "Eight and seven don't add up to 13!"

Randy reflected for a moment and answered back with a smirk, "You're right, coach! And if I'd been as smart as you are, we would have lost the game!"

Where to take it from here...

Sometimes the correct answers are not always the right answers. Certainly when it comes to matters of faith, reason more often than not has to take a backseat. Not that you have to turn your brain off. It's just that the Christian faith rarely makes sense to people unfamiliar with the often upside-down world of Christianity. It was on the cross, of all places, that Jesus actually won the game, so to speak. The Bible says that kind of salvation is foolishness to those who don't believe (1 Corinthians 1:23-25). Wise people know that even though the gospel doesn't add up, the truth of it sets us free.

Sleeping Through the Storm

Years ago a farmer owned land along the Atlantic seacoast. He constantly advertised for hired hands. Most people were reluctant to work on farms along the Atlantic. They dreaded the awful storms that raged across the Atlantic, wreaking havoc on the buildings and crops.

As the farmer interviewed applicants for the job, he received a steady stream of refusals. Finally, a short, thin man, well past middle age, approached the farmer. "Are you a good farmhand?" the farmer asked him.

"Well, I can sleep when the wind blows," answered the little man. Although puzzled by this answer, the farmer, desperate for help, hired him. The little man worked well around the farm, busy from dawn to dusk, and the farmer felt satisfied with the man's work.

Then one night the wind howled loudly in from offshore. Jumping out of bed, the farmer grabbed a lantern and rushed next door to the hired hand's sleeping quarters. He shook the little man and yelled, "Get up! A storm is coming! Tie things down before they blow away!"

The little man rolled over in bed and said firmly, "No sir. I told you, I can sleep when the wind blows."

Enraged by the old man's response, the farmer was tempted to fire him on the spot. Instead, he hurried outside to prepare for the storm. To his amazement, he discovered that all of the haystacks had been covered with tarpaulins. The cows were in the barn, the chickens were in the coops, and the doors were barred. The shutters were tightly secured. Everything was tied down. Nothing could blow away. The farmer then understood what his hired hand meant, and he returned to bed to also sleep while the wind blew.

Where to take it from here...

When you're prepared, you have nothing to fear. Can you sleep when the wind blows through your life? The hired hand in the story was able to sleep because he had secured the farm against the storm. We secure ourselves against the storms of life by grounding ourselves firmly in the Word of God.

34 ———————————— *Still More* Hot Illustrations for Youth Talks

THE TOP 15 BIBLICAL WAYS TO GET A WIFE

Guys! Ever wonder if the Bible has any tips on how to find the girl of your dreams? Good news! There are numerous biblical examples for you to consider:

1. Find an attractive prisoner of war, bring her home, shave her head, trim her nails, and give her new clothes. Then she's yours. (Deuteronomy 21:11-13)
2. Find a prostitute and marry her. (Hosea 1:1-3)
3. Find a man with seven daughters and impress him by watering his flock. (Moses—Exodus 2:16-21)
4. Purchase a piece of property and get a woman as part of the deal. (Boaz—Ruth 4:5-10)
5. Go to a party and hide. When the women come out to dance, grab one and carry her off to be your wife. (Judges 21:19-25)
6. Have God create a wife for you while you sleep. But be careful; it'll cost you a rib (Adam—Genesis 2:19-24)
7. Agree to work seven years in exchange for a woman's hand in marriage. Get tricked into marrying the wrong woman, then work another seven years for the woman you wanted to marry in the first place. That's right. Fourteen years of hard labor for a wife. (Jacob—Genesis 29:15-30)
8. Cut 200 foreskins off the enemies of your future father-in-law and get his daughter in exchange. (David—1 Samuel 18:27)
9. Even if no one is out there, just wander around a bit and you'll find someone. Maybe even your sister. (Cain—Genesis 4:16-17)

(continued)

10. Become the emperor of a huge nation and hold a beauty contest. (Xerxes—Esther 2:3-4)

11. When you see someone you like, go home and tell your parents, "I have seen a woman I like. Now get her for me." If your parents question your decision, simply say, "Get her for me. She's the one for me." (Samson—Judges 14:1-3)

12. Kill any husband and take *his* wife. (David—2 Samuel 11)

13. Wait for your brother to die, then take his widow. It's not just a good idea; it's the law. (Deuteronomy and Leviticus, example of Boaz in Ruth)

14. Don't be so picky. Make up for quality with quantity. (Solomon—1 Kings 11:1-3)

15. A wife?...NOT! (Paul—1 Corinthians 7:32-35)

Where to take it from here...

Obviously, these were not examples you were meant to follow. In fact, several of them would be good examples of what not to do. The Bible is very candid about the failures and follies of God's people.

On the other hand, don't be surprised if God leads you to your mate in a most unusual way! Regardless of how you find the wife (or husband) of your dreams, however, the Bible clearly states the obligations and responsibilities of marriage. It is to be a lifelong commitment between two people who love God, love each other, and have become "one flesh" (Mark 10:8).

A Nobody Named Kimball

Edward Kimball was concerned about one of his young Sunday school students who worked at a shoe store in town. One day Kimball visited him at the store, found the student in the back stocking shoes, and led him to Christ then and there. Dwight L. Moody eventually left the shoe store to become one of the greatest preachers and evangelists of all time.

Moody, whose international speaking took him to the British Isles, preached in a little chapel pastored by a young man with the imposing name of Frederic Brotherton Meyer. In his sermon Moody told an emotionally charged story about a Sunday school teacher he had known in Chicago who personally went to every student in his class and led every one of them to Christ.

That message changed Pastor Meyer's entire ministry, inspiring him to become an evangelist like Moody. Over the years Meyer came to America several times to preach. Once in Northfield, Massachusetts, a confused young preacher sitting in the back row heard Meyer say, "If you are not willing to give up everything for Christ, are you willing to be made willing?" That remark led J. Wilbur Chapman to respond to the call of God on his life.

Chapman went on to become one of the most effective evangelists of his time. A volunteer by the name of Billy Sunday helped set up his crusades and learned how to preach by watching Chapman. Sunday eventually took over Chapman's ministry, becoming one of the most dynamic evangelists of the 20th century. In the great arenas of the nation, Billy Sunday's preaching turned thousands of people to Christ.

Inspired by a 1924 Billy Sunday crusade in Charlotte, North Carolina, a committee of Christians there dedicated themselves to reaching that city for Christ. The committee invited the evangelist Mordecai Ham to hold a series of evangelistic meetings in 1932. A lanky 16-year-old sat in the huge crowd one evening, spellbound by the message of the white-haired preacher, who seemed to be shouting and waving his lone finger at him. Night after night the teenager attended and finally went forward to give his life to Christ.

The teenager's name? Billy Graham—the man who has undoubtedly communicated the gospel of Jesus Christ to more people than any other man in history.

Where to take it from here...

Remember how this sequence of events started? A "nobody" named Kimball, concerned for one of his students, visited him at a shoe store—and in doing that, he changed the world. Millions of people have been affected by his decision to go to that shoe store and share the gospel with one person. And millions more will continue to feel the impact of it.

Can anything like that happen today? You bet it can. God wants to use you to change the world.

Uncle George

The children of a well-to-do family decided to give their father a book containing their family's history for a birthday present. They commissioned a professional biographer to write the book, carefully cautioning him about the family's "black sheep"—their Uncle George had been executed in the electric chair for murder, and they felt that it would be best if the biographer left Uncle George out of the book.

"No need to do that," said the biographer. "I can report the situation in such a way that there will be no embarrassment to your father or to you. I'll merely write that Uncle George occupied a chair of applied electronics at an important government institution. He was attached to his position by the strongest ties, and his death came as a real shock."

Where to take it from here...

How would a biographer write about your life? Would he have to disguise the truth? What do you think people might say about you after you die? Answering questions like these will help you recognize the kind of life you're living right now.

The Bible teaches us that when you die, there's nothing else you can do to get ready to meet God (Hebrews 9:27). It won't matter what people write about you or say about you to make you look good (or look better than you actually were). God knows all about you, and you will be judged by him.

Well, Nobody's Perfect

Imagine you're on your church's search committee, investigating applicants desiring to pastor your congregation. Among the letters from candidates is the following letter:

Dear Brothers and Sisters in Christ,

Grace and peace to you from God our Father and from the Lord Jesus Christ. Understanding that your pulpit is vacant, I'd like to be considered for the job. You see, I love to preach, even though my preaching tends to stir up quite a bit of controversy. In fact, one of my sermons caused a riot. Actually, I've never been able to stay in one place more than three years.

My health isn't too good. I have what I call a "thorn in the flesh—and to be perfectly honest, I'm not much to look at. I can assure you, however, that this doesn't interfere with my ministry. I'm a bachelor by choice—never been married and never had any kids—but I'm surprisingly good at conducting family life seminars.

If you do a background check on me—and I'm sure you will—you'll probably discover that I changed my name a while back, and I have been arrested a few times. But even in jail I was able to have a successful ministry. People tell me I'm quite a theologian, although I've never attended seminary.

I hope you aren't looking for an administrator. I'm not too good at keeping records. And my memory's not too good. Sometimes I forget who I've baptized, for instance. But I'm a hard worker, although the things I want to do, I rarely do. And the things I don't want to do, I always end up doing. Go figure. But you know what? I've found that everything works out fine in the end for those who love God and are called according to his purpose. Praise be to God.

Well, let me know if you are interested. I can start next week. By the way, I wrote this with my own hand.

Grace to you all,

Paul

Where to take it from here...

Would you call the Apostle Paul to pastor a church? God did.

If God could use Paul, chances are he can use you. Remarkable talent and physical perfection are not prerequisites to being used by God. Most of the heroes of the Bible, in fact, were imperfect, inexperienced, unqualified—certainly not the kind of people we would have chosen to do the job. Their inadequacy, however, motivated them to depend upon God and to follow him in obedience. When you think you "have it all together," you tend do things your way instead of God's way. God isn't waiting for you to get good enough to serve him. He's waiting instead for you to say yes.

CHIP AND DALE'S BIG PUSH

Disney's Chip and Dale always get the best of Donald Duck. In one cartoon those pesky chipmunks are taunting him from their little tree hole about fifteen feet above the ground. Putting on some spiked shoes, Donald Duck attempts to climb the tree. Fuming and muttering, he reaches the hole. In a flash Chip and Dale untie his shoes, and he falls to the ground.

Next he tries using a ladder. When he reaches the top, though, Chip and Dale push the ladder over and Donald tumbles down. For his third assault on the tree, he straps a rocket on his back and launches toward the top of the tree. No use. Chip and Dale jolt the rocket off course, and it crashes with Donald Duck still attached.

Finally, Donald Duck decides to chop the tree down. With steam coming out of his ears, he snatches a big ax and starts swinging. Every time the ax hits the tree, Chip and Dale shake in their perch. In agitated chatter they wonder how to save themselves this time.

Meanwhile, the tree begins to fall, and Donald Duck quacks with glee, certain of his success. Then, for no apparent reason, the tree not only stops falling, but it begins to right itself again. A furious Donald circles the tree trying to figure out the reason why.

The cartoonist reveals it all. Inside the hollow tree trunk, Chip and Dale are pushing with all their might to upright the tree.

Where to take it from here...

We laugh because it's physically impossible to push a tree up from inside the tree. You've got to brace yourself against something.

Then again, perhaps Chip and Dale did have something to brace themselves against—their desire to survive. At one or more times in your life, you will have nothing to lean against or rely upon except your faith in God and your desire to survive. That's when God is able to do the impossible.

The Littlest Candle

Once upon a time a little candle stood in a room filled with other candles, most of them much larger and much more beautiful than she was. Some were ornate and some were rather simple, like herself. Some were white, some were blue, some were pink, some were green. She had no idea why she was there, and the other candles made her feel rather small and insignificant.

When the sun went down and the room began to get dark, she noticed a large man walking toward her with a ball of fire on a stick. She suddenly realized that the man was going to set her on fire. "No, no!!" she cried, "Aaaaagghhh! Don't burn me, please!" But she knew that she could not be heard and prepared for the pain that would surely follow.

To her surprise, the room filled with light. She wondered where it came from since the man had extinguished his fire stick. To her delight, she realized that the light came from herself.

Then the man struck another fire stick and, one by one, lit the other candles in the room. Each one gave out the same light that she did.

During the next few hours, she noticed that, slowly, her wax began to flow. She became aware that she would soon die. With this realization came a sense of why she had been created. "Perhaps my purpose on earth is to give out light until I die," she mused. And that's exactly what she did.

Where to take it from here...

God created you and I to produce light in a dark world. Like that little candle, we all can produce the same amount of light, no matter how small we are or what color we might be. But we can't produce light until we receive it from an outside source. That source is Jesus Christ, the light of the world.

Also like the little candle, we have to die in order to produce light. If we try to preserve ourselves, our lives will be meaningless. But if we are willing to lose our lives for Christ's sake (Matthew 10:39), we will find our true purpose and meaning.

The Polish Underground

A fighter in the Polish underground resistance movement from 1939 to 1944, Mr. Stypulkowski was captured by the Russian army at the end of the war. He and 15 other Poles were taken to Russia to stand trial for treason. Since these Polish "double-agents" had in fact helped to defeat the Nazis, the prosecutors had no evidence that they aided the enemy. The only way to convict them would be to get them to make a full confession.

Prior to the trial, guards rigorously interrogated the men, attempting to break them mentally, emotionally, and spiritually—to destroy their integrity—so they would confess to anything demanded of them. Fifteen of the 16 men broke under the grueling pressure. Only Stypulkowski held out. He endured 69 nights of brutal questioning in a series of 141 interrogations. At one point even his interrogator had a mental breakdown and had to be replaced. Relentlessly his tormentors examined everything he had done, or hadn't done, to find anything that could be used against him. They found plenty of dirt—Stypulkowski was no saint—but they were unable to extract a confession for the crimes of which he was being accused.

Starved, sleep-deprived, and in constant terror, Stypulkowski resisted even in the face of the signed confessions of his best friends blaming him for their trouble. His torturers told him his case was hopeless and as good as closed. They advised him to plead guilty so they could lessen his sentence; otherwise, he could expect certain death. But Stypulkowski continued refusing to make the full confession they wanted. He confidently stated that he had not been a traitor and could not confess to something which was not true. Throughout all these horrors he kept his Christian faith vital by regular prayer. He subordinated every other loyalty to his loyalty to Christ. Most impressive of all was the completely natural way that he witnessed about his faith.

At his trial he pled "not guilty," expecting to pay for the rebellion with his life. However, mainly because of the western observers who attended the trial, the Russians reluctantly dropped the charges against Stypulkowski and he was freed.

Where to take it from here...

Stypulkowski endured because he daily presented himself to God and to his accusers in absolute honesty. Knowing he was accepted and loved by God, forgiven and cleansed by his Savior, he freely admitted to all the wrongdoing his enemies uncovered from his past. "I never felt it necessary to justify myself with excuses," he recalls. "When they showed me I was a coward, I already knew it. When they shook their fingers at me with accusations of filthy, lewd feelings, I already knew it. When they showed me a reflection of myself with all my inadequacies, I said to them, 'But gentlemen, I am much worse than that.' For you see, I had learned it was unnecessary for me to justify myself; One had already done that for me—Jesus Christ!" He could freely admit his personal failures because he knew they had all been taken care of at the Cross.

All who have that kind of faith in Jesus Christ are also justified—"we have peace with God through our Lord Jesus Christ, through whom we have gained access by faith into this grace in which we now stand" (Romans 5:1–2). Counting on God's justifying grace, we can find the courage to face the truth about ourselves and experience healing.

Where Did I Come From?

A little boy had to write a report for school, so he went to his mother and asked, "Mom, where did I come from?"

Surprised at hearing such a question from her child, the mother discreetly answered, "Um, the stork brought you."

"And where did YOU come from?" the boy continued.

"Well, the stork brought me, just like he brought you. Now go to your room. No more questions, please."

But the boy persisted. "What about grandma? Where did grandma come from?"

"Look, the stork brought grandma, the stork brought me, the stork brought you! Now go to your room. I do not want to talk about this any more!"

So the little boy went to his room and began writing his report.

"Our family hasn't had a normal birth in three generations..."

Where to take it from here...

Do you ever wonder how you got here? The world sometimes gives you answers that are about as stupid as "the stork brought you." Don't believe it. You didn't get here by accident. You're not just a highly developed monkey. The Bible tells us that you were "fearfully and wonderfully made" (Psalm 139:14).

Reducing the mysteries of the universe to something that we can measure is like parents telling small children tall tales so they'll stop asking questions. Don't let tall tales invented in the name of science rob you of your faith. No one knows exactly how God did it, but we know that God created everything, including you and I—and he knows each of us by name. Not only that, he loves and desires a personal relationship with each person he has created. He wants to have a personal relationship with you.

Santa's Trip

"Yes Virginia, there is a Santa Claus."

It is truly heartwarming to know that millions of people around the world believe in Santa. Sure, most are under four feet tall, but still it's amazing that so many believe in the big guy in the red suit. Consider the following:

Around the globe, today, live approximately two billion children (persons under 18). Santa doesn't visit all of them, of course. Subtracting the number of Muslim, Hindu, Jewish, or Buddhist children reduces Santa's Christmas Eve work load to 15 percent of the total, or 378 million children (according to the Population Reference Bureau). At an average (census) rate of 3.5 children per household, and presuming that there is at least one good child in each home, Santa must visit about 108 million homes.

Santa has about 31 hours of Christmas to work with, thanks to the different time zones and the rotation of the earth, assuming he travels east to west (which seems logical). This works out to 967.7 visits per second. That means that at each household with a good child, Santa has around 1/1000th of a second to park the sleigh, hop out, jump down the chimney, fill the stockings, distribute the remaining presents under the tree, eat whatever snacks have been left for him, get back up the chimney, jump into the sleigh, and get on to the next house.

For the purposes of our calculations, we will assume that each of these 108 million stops is evenly distributed around the earth (which, of course, we know to be false). We're talking about a trip of 0.78 miles per household; a total trip of 75.5 million miles, not counting bathroom stops or breaks. To cover that ground in 31 hours, Santa's sleigh moves at 650 miles per second—3,000 times the speed of sound. By comparison, the fastest man-made vehicle, the Ulysses space probe, moves at a poky 27.4 miles per second, and a conventional reindeer can run (at best) 15 miles per hour.

The payload of the sleigh adds another interesting element. Assuming that each child gets nothing more than a medium-sized Lego set (two pounds), the sleigh must carry over 500 thousand tons, not counting Santa

himself. On land, a conventional reindeer can pull no more than 300 pounds. In air, even granting that the "flying" reindeer could pull 10 times the normal amount, the job can't be done with a mere eight or nine of them—Santa would need 360,000 of them. This increases the payload, not counting the weight of the sleigh, another 54,000 tons, or roughly seven times the weight of the *Queen Elizabeth* (the ship, not the monarch).

$$E = MC^2 \times \frac{BQ}{\sqrt{.04}} > \pi \cdot 3$$

Six hundred thousand tons traveling at 650 miles per second creates enormous air resistance—this would heat up the reindeer in the same fashion as a spacecraft reentering the earth's atmosphere. The lead pair of reindeer would absorb 14.3 quintillion joules of energy per second each. In short, they would burst into flames almost instantaneously, exposing the reindeer behind them and creating deafening sonic booms in their wake. The entire reindeer team would be vaporized within 4.26 thousandths of a second, or right about the time Santa reached the fifth house on his trip.

Not that it matters, however, since Santa, as a result of accelerating from a dead stop to 650 miles per second in .001 seconds, would be subjected to centrifugal forces of 17,500 g's. A 250-pound Santa (which seems ludicrously slim) would be pinned to the back of the sleigh by 4,315,015 pounds of force, instantly crushing his bones and organs and reducing him to a quivering blob of pink goo.

Where to take it from here...

Considering all this, it's amazing that some children (and even a few adults) have no problem believing in Santa. By comparison, the story of the little baby in the manger is relatively easy to believe. The life of Jesus Christ is a fact, recorded not only by biblical writers but by secular historians as well. Some historians declare that there is more evidence for the birth, death, and resurrection of Christ than there is evidence that Julius Caesar ever lived at all.

Even in the face of the written testimony of eyewitnesses, many people refuse to believe in Jesus. They consider him nothing more than a myth. But for those willing to believe with childlike faith, Jesus promises an inheritance of the kingdom of God (Mark 10:14).

THE PRIZE

A billionaire oil tycoon from Texas decided to find a husband for his only daughter, a rather homely 18-year-old. He initiated his search by inviting local bachelors to a party in his backyard. A large, elegantly designed swimming pool dominated the yard. As the men edged by it to get their refreshments, they saw it was filled with man-eating sharks, piranhas, alligators, and other animals that wouldn't think twice about eating you alive. Clustering beside the pool, the bachelors puzzled over the strange sight.

Just then the tycoon appeared on the patio and gave an emotional speech, telling how much he loved his daughter and expressing how much he wanted her to marry someone deserving of her. He then laid out The Deal.

"Anyone who will jump in the swimming pool and swim to the other side will have their choice of a check for one million dollars with no questions asked or the title deed to my most profitable oil field or the hand of my daughter in marriage and your place in my will, which will result in your inheriting my entire fortune."

The bachelors were speechless. Their questioning looks seemed to say that none of them would be crazy enough to risk his life—even for all that money.

The long silence was finally broken by a splash. Everyone turned to see one of the men swimming to the far side of the pool as fast as any Olympic swimmer. Leaping out of the water, he shook himself and stalked back to the tycoon. With a hug and a handshake, the tycoon congratulated the young man on a fine swim. "Son, would you like a million dollar check?" he asked.

"No sir, I wouldn't," responded the young man politely, and slightly out of breath.

"Fine," said the tycoon. "Then would you like my most profitable oil field?"

"No sir," he replied, getting a hold on himself.

(continued)

With a tear in his eye the tycoon asked, "Then, my boy, would you like my only daughter's hand in marriage?"

To the surprise of the gawking bachelors, the young man replied, "No sir."

Puzzled and a little hurt, the tycoon asked, "Well then, son, what *do* you want?"

"I only want one thing," answered the young man with assurance. "I want the name of the guy who pushed me in the pool."

Where to take it from here...

Nobody would willingly jump into a shark-infested pool—even for a million dollars. And nobody would willingly let themselves be nailed to a Roman cross—even if he thought he might get some fame or recognition out of it.

Jesus let himself be nailed to that cross, not because there was something in it for him personally, but because there was something in it for you and me. Jesus did more than risk his life for us; Jesus gave his life for us. Nobody pushed him into it; he chose to die because he loves us.

Still More Hot Illustrations for Youth Talks

Dumb Crooks

Actual crimes committed by actual criminals:

- Two Kentucky men tried to pull off the front of a cash machine by running a chain from the machine to the bumper of their pickup truck. The front panel of the machine was so secure that instead they pulled off the bumper of their truck. Scared, they fled the scene and drove home, leaving the chain attached to the machine...with their bumper still attached to the chain...with their vehicle's license plate still attached to the bumper.

- A man convicted of robbery in Texas worked out a deal to pay $9,600 in damages rather than serve a prison sentence. For payment he provided the court with a check—a stolen check with a forged signature. He got 10 years.

- A man went into a drugstore, pulled a gun, announced a robbery, and pulled a Hefty trash-bag face mask over his head. Too late he realized that he'd forgotten to cut eyeholes in the mask. While sprinting blindly to the door, he fell down and was captured.

- A man successfully broke into a bank after hours and stole—are you ready for this?—the bank's video camera...while it was recording...remotely. In other words, he got a camera only. The video-tape of himself stealing the camera was still in the *recorder* located elsewhere in the bank.

- A man successfully broke into a bank's basement through a street-level window, cutting himself up pretty badly in the process. He then realized that he couldn't get to the money from where he was, and he couldn't climb back out the window through which he had entered. On top of that he was bleeding from all his cuts. So he located a phone and dialed 911 for help.

- A man walked into a convenience store, put a $20 bill on the counter, and asked for change. When the clerk opened the cash drawer, the man pulled a gun and demanded all the cash in the register, which the clerk promptly provided. The man grabbed the cash from the clerk and fled—leaving the $20 bill on the counter. The total amount of cash he got from the drawer? Fifteen dollars.

- In San Francisco a man walked into a downtown Bank of America and wrote, "This is a stickup. Put all your many in this bag." While standing in line waiting to give his note to the teller, he began to worry that someone had seen him write the note and might call the police before he reached the teller window. So he left the Bank of America and crossed the street to Wells Fargo.

   After waiting a few minutes in line, he handed his note to the Wells Fargo teller. She read it and, guessing from his spelling errors that he was not the brightest bank robber in the world, told him that she could not accept his stickup note because it was written on a Bank of America deposit slip and that he would either have to fill out a Wells Fargo deposit slip or go back to Bank of America.

   Looking somewhat defeated, the man said okay and left the Wells Fargo Bank. The Wells Fargo teller then called the police, who arrested him a few minutes later as he was waiting in line back at the Bank of America.

Where to take it from here...

Sin is stupid.

Still More **Hot Illustrations for Youth Talks**

ALL IS FORGIVEN

In his short story "The Capital of the World," Ernest Hemingway tells the story of a Spanish father and his teenage son. The relationship between this father and son became strained and eventually shattered. When the rebellious son—whose name was Paco, a common Spanish name—ran away from home, his father began a long and arduous search to find him. As a last resort the exhausted father placed an ad in a Madrid newspaper, hoping that his son would see the ad and respond to it. The ad read,

Dear Paco,

Please meet me in front of the newspaper office at noon. All is forgiven.

Love,
Father

As Hemingway tells the story, the next day at noon, in front of the newspaper office, there were 800 Pacos, all seeking forgiveness from their fathers.

Where to take it from here...

Are you like one of those Pacos? Carrying around a load of guilt, wanting forgiveness, but not knowing where to find it? Your Father in heaven, who loves you very much, has made the first move. Just as Paco's father ran an ad in the paper, so God sent his son to die on a Roman cross.

"If I am lifted up," Jesus said, talking about the Cross, "I will draw all men to myself" (John 12:32). And along with all those Pacos who showed up at the newspaper office, you're invited to come as well.

Still More Hot Illustrations for Youth Talks ———————— **53**

The Street Bum

One night at a small church in Atlanta, Georgia, a man shared how he had become a Christian while in Sydney, Australia. "I was at the street corner in Kings Cross," the man began, "when I felt a tug on my sleeve. Turning, I found myself face to face with a street bum. Before I could say anything, the man simply asked me, 'Mister, if you were to die tonight, where would you spend eternity?' That question troubled me over the next three weeks," the man continued. "I had to find an answer, and I ended up giving my life to Christ."

The pastor of the Atlanta church was amazed that a man on a street corner could have such an impact. But imagine his amazement when, three years later, another man came to his church and gave an almost identical testimony. He, too, had been at Kings Cross in Sydney when a derelict had pulled on his sleeve and then asked him, "If you were to die tonight, where would you spend eternity?" This second man, also haunted by the street bum's question, eventually sought and found an answer in Jesus.

Shortly after hearing the second testimony, the pastor of that small church in Atlanta had to be in Sydney for a missions conference. On one of his nights off, he went to Kings Cross to see if he could find the man who had been mentioned at his church by two different people. Pausing on a street corner to look for someone like the street bum he'd heard about, he felt a tug at his jacket. He turned, and before the poor old man could say anything, the pastor blurted out, "I know what you're going to ask me! You're going to ask me if I were to die tonight, where would I spend eternity?"

The man was stunned. "How did you know that?" he inquired.

The pastor told him the whole story. When he finished, the man started to cry. "Mister," he said, "10 years ago I gave my life to Jesus, and I wanted to do something for him. But a man like me can't do much of anything. So I decided I would just hang out on this corner and ask people that simple question. I've been doing that for years, mister, but tonight is the first time I ever knew it did anybody any good."

God calls us not to be successful, but to be faithful. We need to obey God even though we can't see whether it does any good. When you share Christ with someone, for instance, or when you help a person in need, you aren't responsible for the outcome. It's God's job to form us into what we can be in Christ.

On the other side of things, be careful not to judge others for what they are doing in the Kingdom of God, even when it seems foolish or unproductive. God uses all kinds of ministry in many different ways in order to fulfill his purposes. Just because you don't get the point of a particular ministry doesn't mean it's wrong or worthless.

TAKE ME TO YOUR LEADER

An Austrian army commander was ordered to lay siege to a small village in the Tyrol. His army had met stubborn resistance in that part of the country, but the advantage was clearly his. He knew that it was just a matter of time before he emerged victorious.

His confidence was shaken, however, when one of his prisoners remarked, "You will never take Tyrol, for they have an invincible leader!"

"What's he talking about?" the commander inquired of his staff. "Who is this leader of whom he speaks?" No one seemed to know, so the commander dismissed the comment. Paid little attention to it. Being a cautious leader, however, he doubled his preparations for the attack on the village—just in case.

As his army descended through the pass in the Alps, the commander noticed cattle still grazing in the valley and people working in the fields as if nothing were going to happen.

Either they are not expecting us, or this is a trap! thought the commander. He continued marching towards the village with colors flying, horns sounding a challenge, and weapons drawn. Although the commotion brought women and children to their doorways, no one panicked. Instead, the people of the village quietly returned to their household chores as if the threatening army meant no harm to them at all.

The commander found it increasingly difficult to maintain order within his troops. Some of the soldiers were answering questions from the children. One old warrior blew a kiss to a little girl standing on a doorstep. "She looks just like my little Lisa," he commented.

All his senses alerted, the commander still found no sign of ambush. When the troops stood in the open square at the center of the village, facing the town hall, he fully expected the battle to begin. An old white-haired man, apparently the mayor, emerged from the town hall, followed by 10 men in simple peasant clothes. Carrying no weapons, the dignified group stood in the square, unimpressed by the huge armed force before them—the most terrible soldiers in the great and mighty army of Austria.

"Welcome, brother!" said the old man to the commander as he extended his hand. One of the soldiers immediately drew his sword, prepared to strike the man dead if he came any closer. But clearly the old man meant no harm.

"Where are your soldiers?" demanded the commander of the mayor.

"Soldiers? We have no soldiers." replied the old man with a puzzled look, as if the commander had asked "Where are your elephants?"

"But we have come to take your village!" shouted the commander.

"Well, no one will stop you," replied the old man.

"Are there none here to fight us?" asked the commander.

"No, there is no one here to fight. We have chosen Christ for our leader, and he has taught us another way."

The commander knew no military strategy for this kind of confrontation. After consulting with his lead officers, the commander retreated from the village with his troops, leaving it untouched.

The commander later wrote in his journal, "The village was impossible to take. Had I ordered my men to fire on those smiling men, women, and children, I knew they would not have obeyed me. Even military discipline has its limits. Could I command a soldier to shoot down a child who reminded him of his Lisa? I reported to headquarters that the town had offered unassailable resistance, although this admission damaged my military reputation. But I was right. We had been conquered by these simple folk who followed implicitly the leadership of Jesus Christ."

Where to take it from here...

The way of Jesus taught in the Sermon on the Mount (Matthew 5-7) still baffles people today. Yet his teaching holds true. Jesus taught his followers to love their enemies and to pray for them rather than to take up arms. Not many Christians have taken those words seriously. What do you think would happen if we did?

The Day of the Rabbit

In his book *A Severe Mercy,* author Sheldon Vanauken tells the story of a dog named Gypsy.

Gypsy was a furry, wheat-colored collie who lived and played on a ranch—several hundred acres of hills and woods, full of good things like rabbit trails and streams. She loved it there. At the ranch house she was given a comfortable bed and good meals. Her Master, who owned the ranch, made no unreasonable demands on her. She knew that her job was to love her Master and to be faithful to him and to obey other commands—to follow, to come, to lie down. And she also knew that she wasn't supposed to chase the chickens and the rabbits. Actually these were easy for Gypsy, because it was in her nature to obey and to love her Master.

But one day when Gypsy was prowling on a hill far away, past the spring house and pasture, two things happened at once: the Master called her and a rabbit dashed across the hill. Gypsy turned and raced towards the Master, as she had always done. Then she stopped. It entered her mind that she didn't have to obey. Perhaps the Master didn't understand about that rabbit. Anyway, these were *her* hills. The rabbit was hers, too. Very likely it was all lies—that story of everything, including herself, belonging to the Master. How did she know that the food in her dish came from him? Probably there was some natural explanation. She was a free dog and that was the end of it. These thoughts went through her mind swiftly while she stood irresolute. Again came the Master's command; the rabbit crossed the hilltop. Gypsy whirled and raced after the rabbit. She had made a choice. She was free to choose.

Hours later she came home. She saw the Master waiting for her, but she did not rush gladly to him, leaping and frisking as she had always done. Something new came into her demeanor: guilt. She crept up to him like a snake on her belly. Undoubtedly she was penitent at the moment. But she had a new knowledge—the knowledge of the possibility of sin—and it was a thrill in her heart and a salt taste in her mouth. Nevertheless she was very obedient the next day and the day after that. Eventually, though, there was another rabbit, and she didn't even hesitate.

The Master still loved her, but he trusted her no longer. He put Gypsy in a pen and took her for walks with a rope around her neck. All her real freedom was gone. But the Master gave her, from time to time, new chances to obey of her own free will. Had she chosen to obey, she would have once again had perfect freedom to roam her hundreds of acres. But she did not. She always chose, if she were out of reach, to run away. The Master, knowing that hunger would eventually bring her back, let her run. He could have stopped her. A rifle shot would have ended her rebellion once and for all. But she was allowed to live. Perhaps she would someday choose the way of obedience and true freedom.

One day, during a journey by car, Gypsy and her young daughter Flurry were taken to the edge of the woods. Always before, Gypsy had limited her disobedience to the ranch. But now, coming back to the car, she suddenly felt the old thrill. She turned and ran away. The Master called with a note of sharp urgency. Flurry, in her innocence, came at once. But Gypsy, her ears dulled to the voice of the Master, continued her rush into the dark forest. After hours of searching and calling, the Master sadly abandoned the lost dog and with Flurry beside him, went home.

Flurry continued to live in freedom, always being obedient to the Master who loved her and took good care of her. She was happy to be in his service and she loved the look on his face when she did something that pleased him. She obeyed gladly of her own free choice.

But lost Gypsy, as long as she still lived, wandered the woods and roads as an outcast. She had lost her way home. She became dirty and matted with foxtails and thorns. Stones were often thrown at her, and she was always hungry. She had more puppies who, like her, were lost and inclined to disobedience—as were their puppies for generations to come. The kind and benevolent hand of the Master was unknown to them, except as a tale.

But this is the way Gypsy chose on the Day of the Rabbit, and continued to choose, until finally there was no more choosing left to do.

(continued)

God created Adam and Eve with complete freedom—freedom not only to enjoy all that God had given them, but freedom to choose to obey or to disobey. We all know how they chose.

Adam and Eve, filled with guilt over their disobedience, covered themselves and hid from God. Their innocence was gone, and they could no longer be trusted. God had to place them and their offspring under tighter restrictions called the Law. But still they disobeyed, and all of their offspring—that's us—have inherited their tendency to disobey. "All have sinned and fall short of the glory of God" (Romans 3:23).

That's why Jesus came. If the Master in this story could have actually become a dog and chased Gypsy through the woods to bring her back, that would approximate what God did when he sent Jesus.

God continues to call us back, and we still have the freedom to choose the way of obedience over the way of sin and death. The Bible says, "Choose for yourselves this day whom you will serve" (Joshua 24:15). We can use our free will to choose the way of obedience. And when we do, God gives us even more freedom to enjoy life to its fullest. Jesus said, "I have come that they may have life, and have it to the full" (John 10:10). The way of sin and disobedience robs you of your freedom. Don't be a slave to sin. Choose Jesus Christ and you will have more freedom than you ever knew was possible.

Finding Happiness in Tibet

A bright young premed student from Harvard University journeyed to the mountains of Tibet during the summer following his sophomore year. There he met a monk who said to him, "Don't you see how you are poisoning your soul with your success-oriented way of life? Your idea of happiness is to stay up all night studying for an exam so you can get a better grade than your friend. Your idea of a happy marriage is not finding a woman who will make you whole, but winning the girl that everyone else wants. That's not how people are supposed to live. Life is not a competition. Give it up. Come join us in an atmosphere where we share, live in harmony, and love one another. Here you can find true happiness."

The young man had completed four years at a competitive high school to get into Harvard and had worked hard to become one of the top premed students in his class at the university. He was ripe for the appeal of the Tibetan monk. He called his parents and told them that he would not be coming home. He was dropping out of school to live in a Buddhist monastery.

Six months later, he wrote his parents: "Dear Mom and Dad, I know you weren't happy with the decision I made last summer, but I want to tell you that I am doing great. For the first time in my life, I am at peace. Here there is no competing, no hustling, no trying to get ahead of anyone else. Here we are all equal, and we all share. This way of life is so much in harmony with the inner essence of my soul that in only six months I've become the number two disciple in the entire monastery, and I think I can become number one by June!"

Where to take it from here...

Obviously, nothing changed for this young man except his environment. On the inside he remained the same person, and he will probably be as discontent as he was before when the novelty of living in a new place wears off.

You can't find happiness or peace simply by changing your external surroundings. What you need is a change on the inside, and that can only happen by giving your life to Jesus Christ. Scripture teaches us that when you become a Christian, "the old is gone, the new has come" (2 Corinthians 5:17). The transformation is complete, from the inside out.

The Flat Tire

Two students were taking organic chemistry at the university. Having done well in their work and labs, they were both going into the final exam with solid A's. So far so good. Trouble was, they were so confident that they decided to party the night before the big test. It was a great night; one thing led to another, and they ended up sleeping late the following morning.

They missed the exam! Disasterville!

Being inventive souls, though, they went to see the professor to explain that they had been visiting a sick, out-of-town friend the night before. On the way home they had a flat tire. With no spare tire and no car jack, they were stranded. They could only manage to hitch a lift back to town midmorning, which is why they missed the test. They were really sorry to have missed the exam, they said (they were so looking forward to it!) but wondered whether they might be able to take it that afternoon.

The professor thought about it for a moment and decided that this would be permissible since they hadn't had time to discuss the exam with any of the students who had already taken it. After a short break for lunch, the two students were ready for the test. The professor placed them in separate rooms, handed each of them an exam booklet, and told them to begin.

Page one, question one. A simple one for five points. This will be easy! Having answered the first question each of the students turned the page for question number two:

It read: "Which tire?" (95 points).

(continued)

Where to take it from here...

The first thing those students realized when they saw the final question was that their professor wasn't nearly as stupid as they thought he was. Second, they realized that they were caught in a lie with no way out.

If you've ever been caught in a lie, you already know that lying makes it impossible for anyone to trust you. The Bible emphatically urges honesty. The admonition to tell the truth is one of the Ten Commandments. Jesus taught that "the truth will set you free" (John 8:32).

NEVER TOO LATE

On June 8, 1972, a nine-year-old Vietnamese girl, her clothes flaming from gasoline bombs, fled the American-led assault on her village of Trang Bang. With her eyes screwed shut and her mouth spread wide in a scream of pain, she was captured on film in America's most remembered Vietnam wartime photo.

In Officer John Plummer's nightmares, this picture flashed huge, in black and white, to a sound track of children screaming. His order had directed bombers to shower Kim Phuc's village with the chemical explosives. For years, guilt over destroying and maiming the villagers haunted the officer. Women and alcohol were his escape of choice.

Twenty years after the destruction of the village, Officer Plummer asked Christ to take control of his life, unleashing God's ultimate power to end guilt. Although free from guilt, he carried inside himself scars somehow linked to the thick, white scars on the neck, arm, and back of the now-grown Vietnamese girl. Six years later, Plummer knew he needed to find her. In an effort to meet her face to face, he tracked her down while she was visiting America.

Unlike the June 1972 event, no photographer captured the moment when Plummer explained to Kim Phuc who he was. But in the middle of a busy sidewalk, the soldier, now 49 years old, and the child, now 33 years old, embraced. "She just opened her arms to me," Plummer later said. "I fell into her arms sobbing. All I could say is, 'I'm so sorry. I'm just so sorry.'"

"It's all right," she replied as she patted Plummer's back. "I forgive. I forgive."

Where to take it from here...

Nothing you've ever done is too bad to ask forgiveness for. And with God, it's never too late to ask for forgiveness. God waits patiently for you to come to him and to ask forgiveness for your sins. Because of what Christ has done for us, God "is faithful and just to forgive us, and to cleanse us from our sins" (1 John 1:9). That's the only way we can have the peace that accompanies freedom from sin.

And when we have been forgiven by God, we are then able to forgive others, and to seek forgiveness from those we have wronged. Jesus taught us to forgive so that we might also be forgiven (Luke 6:37). When we forgive and seek forgiveness, we allow our memories to be healed and we demonstrate the forgiveness that we have received from God.

Get a Bigger Frying Pan

Two men went fishing. One man was an experienced fisherman, the other wasn't. Every time the experienced fisherman caught a big fish, he put it in his ice chest to keep it fresh. Whenever the inexperienced fisherman caught a big fish, he threw it back.

The experienced fisherman watched this go on all day and finally got tired of seeing this man waste good fish. "Why do you keep throwing back all the big fish you catch?" he asked.

The inexperienced fisherman replied, "I only have a small frying pan."

Where to take it from here...

Sometimes, like that fisherman, we throw back the big plans, big dreams, big jobs, big opportunities that God gives us. Our faith is too small. We laugh at that fisherman who didn't figure out that all he needed was a bigger frying pan; yet how ready are we to increase the size of our faith?

Whether it's a problem or a possibility, God will never give you anything bigger than you can handle. That means we can confidently walk into anything God brings our way. You can do all things through Christ (Philippians 4:13).

Nothing is too big for God.

Sewing the Sheets

The women of a New York church, eager to help a missionary newly assigned to an Indian leper colony, were thrilled with the mountains of fabric spread before them. For four weeks they had collected old sheets from the people at their church and carefully cut each sheet into eight inch strips. Finally, they packaged and mailed the fabric. The new missionary could distribute them as bandages for the Indian lepers.

Two weeks later the sheet fragments arrived in India, and the American missionary joyfully passed them out to his new Indian friends. Delighted, the men and women of the leper colony gathered together with all of their new fabric bandages. One woman held up a the fabric strip and enthusiastically proclaimed, "You know, if we sew these together we'll have pretty good sheets."

Where to take it from here...

When we serve others, we need to take time to gain an accurate understanding of their real needs. Jumping to conclusions can lead us to do the wrong things—our faulty assumptions and agendas have nothing to do with the real life of those we desire to serve. The first step in effective ministry of the gospel is to listen.

Table for Two

He sits by himself at a table for two. The uniformed waiter appears at his side.

"Would you like to go ahead and order, sir?" The man has, after all, been waiting since seven o'clock—almost half an hour.

"No, thank you," the man says with a smile. "I'll wait for her a while longer. How about some more coffee?"

"Certainly, sir."

The man sits, his deep brown eyes gazing straight through the flowered centerpiece. He fingers his napkin, allowing the sounds of light chatter, tinkling silverware, and mellow music to fill his mind. Dressed in a sport coat and tie with his dark brown hair neatly combed, he projects a clean-cut and welcoming image. You get the sense that he wants his companion to feel important, respected, loved. Yet he's not so formal as to make one uncomfortable. Having taken every precaution to make others feel at ease with him, still, he sits alone. The waiter returns to fill the man's coffee cup.

"Is there anything else I can get for you, sir?"

"No, thank you." The waiter remains standing at the table. Something tugs at his curiosity.

"I don't mean to pry, but..." His voice trails off. This line of conversation could jeopardize his tip, if not his job.

"Go ahead," the man encourages. His voice is strong, yet sensitive, inviting conversation.

"Why do you bother waiting for her?" the waiter finally asks. This man has been at the restaurant other evenings, always alone, always patient.

"Because she needs me."

"Are you sure?"

"Yes."

"Well, sir, no offense, sir, but assuming that she needs you, she sure isn't acting much like it. She's stood you up three times just this week!"

The man winces, and looks down. "Yes, I know."

(continued)

"Then why do you still come here and wait?"

"Cassie said she'd be here."

"She's said that before," the waiter protests. "I wouldn't put up with it. Why do you?"

Now the man looks up at the waiter with a smile. "Because I love her."

The waiter walks away, wondering how he could love a girl who stands him up three times a week. The man must be crazy, he decides. From across the room he turns to look again at the man, who is pouring cream into his coffee cup. He twirls his spoon between his fingers a few times before stirring sweetener into his cup. After staring for a moment into the liquid, the man brings the cup to his mouth and sips, silently watching those around him. *He doesn't look crazy*, the waiter admits to himself. *Maybe the girl has qualities that I don't know about. Or maybe the man's love is stronger than most.* Pulling himself out of his musings, the waiter moves to take an order from a party of five.

Setting down his coffee cup, the man recalls the many things he wanted to talk over with Cassie. But really he was mostly looking forward to hearing her voice telling him about her day—her triumphs, her defeats...anything. Yes, she's stood him up before, but he still can't get used to it. Each time, it hurts. He's looked forward to the evening all day. He's tried so many times to show Cassie how much he loves her. He'd just like to know that she cares for him, too. He sips sporadically at the coffee. He hopes Cassie may yet arrive.

The clock says nine-thirty when the waiter returns to the man's table—still with one empty chair.

"Anything I can get for you?"

"No, I think that will be all for tonight. May I have the check, please?"

"Yes, sir." When the waiter leaves, the man picks up the check. He pulls out his wallet. He has enough money to have given Cassie a feast. But he takes out only enough to pay for his five cups of coffee and the tip. *Why do you do this, Cassie?* his mind cries as he gets up from the table.

"Good-bye," the waiter says, as the man walks toward the door.

"Good night. Thank you for your service."

"You're welcome, sir," says the waiter softly, for he sees the hurt in the man's eyes that his smile doesn't hide. The man passes a laughing young

70 —————————— *Still More* **Hot Illustrations for Youth Talks**

couple on his way out, and his eyes glisten as he thinks of the good time he and Cassie could have had. He stops at the front and makes reservations for tomorrow. Maybe Cassie will be able to make it, he thinks.

"Seven o'clock tomorrow for a party of two?" the hostess confirms.

"That's right," the man replies.

"Do you think she'll come?" the hostess inquires tentatively. She doesn't mean to be rude, but she has watched the man many times alone at his table for two.

"Someday, yes. And I will be there waiting for her." The man buttons his overcoat and walks out of the restaurant, alone. His shoulders are hunched, but through the windows the hostess can only guess whether they are hunched against the wind or against the man's hurt.

About the time the man steers his car out of the restaurant's parking lot, Cassie falls into her bed. Tired after an evening out with friends, she reaches toward her nightstand to set the alarm.

"Oh, shoot," she says aloud when she sees the note she had scribbled to herself the previous night. "*Seven o'clock p.m.*...and what'd I write here?...oh, yeah, *Spend some time in prayer.* Well, I'll do it tomorrow night for sure."

Besides, she told herself, she needed tonight with her friends—and now she needs her sleep. Tomorrow night will be fine. Jesus will forgive her. She's sure he doesn't mind.

Where to take it from here...

The most important part of daily devotions is showing up. It doesn't matter what you say or do. Just take time every day to spend a little time with the One who loves you and waits patiently for you to come. He wants to tell you how much he loves you.

A Bad Future Investment

Ancient Egyptians fervently believed in an afterlife. So much so that Egyptian burial rituals are the only custom familiar to most moderns. For thousands of years their misguided faith motivated them to build immense tombs with an ingenuity of design, as well as a cost in labor, money, and blood, that still astonishes people.

Over the centuries the Egyptians prepared each other for eternity by mummifying countless people, animals, and even insects. Within a few centuries, Egypt had a critical excess of mummies reverently wrapped in joyful anticipation of the afterlife. With mummies showing up everywhere, later Egyptians got creative. Nineteenth century European travelers exploring Egypt sent home reports of household roofs thatched with mummies or ground mummies used for fertilizer. Hustling Egyptians sent mummies by the ton to Americans who used their linen wrappings to make paper. Even more bizarre, millions of mummies were used in place of scarce timber for Egypt's wood-burning locomotives—a far cry from the destiny that the original embalmers imagined for their beloved departed and a reminder of the fallacy of holding to a well-intentioned but baseless belief.

Where to take it from here...

Ancient Egyptians were right to believe there's life after death, but it's downhill from there. Almost every world religion, in fact, teaches that death is not the end. They go wrong, however, with their belief that we can prepare for eternity through our own efforts.

Many current false religions, cults, and New Age philosophies offer elaborate schemes for achieving eternal life or for managing your reincarnation. The Bible teaches that there's only one way to gain eternal life, though—it's through believing that Jesus Christ gives eternal life to those who have faith in him (John 3:16).

You Call This Justice?

In the name of "justice," some Americans have initiated strange and convoluted lawsuits. Consider the following:

At a recent boxing match a fan drank too much, got into a fight, and ultimately fell down a flight of stairs. His family wanted "justice," so they hired a lawyer and sued. Included in their lawsuit was "Ticket Master," the company that sold the man the ticket to the boxing match.

Then there was the man who bought a four-seated plane. In order to rig the plane so he could fly it from the back seat, he removed the pilot's seat, along with all its safety equipment. The plane crashed and the man's family sued the company that designed and built it. The family won a million dollars, even though the man altered and deliberately misused the original equipment.

In another case a young woman was injured when her fiancé deliberately smashed into her go-cart as they were finishing up their ride around the track. The court ruled that the young man who actually ran into the woman was 85% responsible, the young woman herself was 14% negligent, and the theme park was 1% involved. However, in the interests of "justice," the theme park was required to pay the entire cash judgment.

Where to take it from here...

Shifting responsibility, blaming others, and expecting someone else to pay for our stupidity is common in today's legal system, but someday we will all stand before a truly righteous judge who will accept no excuse and will tolerate no legal jargon. On judgment day you won't be able to sue anyone or blame anyone else for your own sins. You will be called on to account for every sin you have committed—and you can be certain that your sins will condemn you to death (Romans 6:23).

But don't despair! Although you won't be able to blame anyone else for your sins, right now you still have time to accept God's free gift of salvation. Jesus Christ died on the cross to pay the penalty for your sins. He did it, not because a clever lawyer was able to pin your sins on him—he willingly died because he loves you. He died so you could live (Hebrews 9:27, Matthew 12:36, Romans 2:16, 1 Timothy 4:1,8).

HANGING IN THERE

Two frogs fell into a deep cream bowl.
One was a wise and cheery soul;
The other one took a gloomy view
And bade his friend a sad adieu.

Said the other frog with a merry grin,
"I can't get out, but I won't give in!
I'll swim around till my strength is spent,
Then I will die all the more content."

And as he swam, though ever it seemed,
His struggling began to churn the cream
Until on top of pure butter he stopped
And out of the bowl he quickly hopped.

The moral, you ask? Oh it's easily found:
If you can't get out, just keep swimming around.

Where to take it from here...

Hang in there!

A Matter of Perspective

Consider these illustrations of the dramatic difference one's perspective makes:

- Hold a color photograph right in front of your nose. All you see is a blur of colors. As you move the picture away, however, you can distinguish the people in the picture, the buildings, and the background.

  You perceive events in your life the same way. As time passes and the event is further away from your present, your understanding of the experience becomes clearer. Perspective is severely limited when you're too close to an event. All you see is a blur.

- Jason took a trip to New York with some college friends during spring break. One afternoon they all piled into a cab and headed for the Empire State Building. Accelerating into traffic, the driver honked his horn incessantly and careened around corners. To Jason, jammed into the back seat, the ride seemed chaotic and dangerous. A couple of times he felt sure they were all going to die in a head-on collision.

  To his relief the wild ride brought them safely to the Empire State Building. Easing out of the cab on wobbly legs, the friends paid the driver and headed inside the building that used to be the tallest in New York. They endured a long elevator ride and a long flight of steps before reaching the observation deck high above the city.

  Dazzled by the expansive view from the deck, Jason paused to take it in. Moving to the fence railing, he finally looked straight down to the city streets from which he had just come. To his amazement he saw order and design where, only a few minutes before, he had feared for his life. Dozens of yellow taxis moved together, stopping at red lights and going at green ones. He could hear no horns at all. It all looked so safe.

(continued)

Jason was struck with his difference in perspective. Jammed in the cab and immersed in the traffic, he had one view of life. But looking down from the top of one of the world's tallest buildings, he had another.

- A group of men sat playing cards in a warehouse on the edge of town. Some had been dealt pretty good hands, and they were deciding whether to bluff and stay in that hand or to fold. One man sat calmly, looking at his hand. It was unbeatable—he knew that if he could remain calm and keep his poker-faced expression, in a few moments he would win it all and be rich. Unknown to the card players, however, a few moments earlier a jet pilot had ejected from his plane, and the abandoned plane was hurtling toward the warehouse. The man with the unbeatable hand wouldn't even get to play it.

Where to take it from here...

Being human limits our perspective. We can't sort out the whole picture from where we are in life—only God can. That's why, when he was tempted, Jesus looked to God to get the true perspective. Satan took Jesus to the top of a mountain and told him to look down. "Everything you see I will give you," Satan promised. "All the wealth, kingdoms, and power in the world can be yours" (Matthew 4:8). Jesus turned down the offer, however, because he relied on God's accurate view of how things are. Jesus knew that the entire universe was created for him and that God has destined all the kingdoms of earth to one day bow to Jesus.

When your life seems chaotic and out of control, remember that God sees it all from "higher up." What you see of your little world is too limited to give you the true perspective of an event. The Kingdom of God, on the other hand, encompasses the entire universe for all eternity. Let the view from God's eyes direct your choices and feelings throughout your life. "Do not store up for yourselves treasures on earth...but seek first his kingdom" (Matthew 6:19, 33).

The Holy Men

The following is an adaptation of a story that was told by Tolstoy:

Once upon a time there was a bishop whose learning and wisdom brought him great honors. People everywhere praised his ability to preach and teach. His congregation grew, and he gained great respect in his town as a man of God.

Finally his notoriety spread all the way to the halls of the Vatican. He received word that the Pope would very much like an audience with this great spiritual giant. The town was enthusiastic about this unprecedented opportunity for one of their own. The bishop, too, felt his sense of self-importance swell. When the day of departure arrived, the townspeople swarmed to the docks to see him and his entourage off to Rome.

The weather and winds were with the ship as she sailed off. After a few days of travel, the captain pointed out to the bishop a tiny island off in the distance. "That," he said, "is the home of the three hermits." (In those days some people had chosen to cut themselves off from all of society in order to better serve and love God.) "It is said that they are the holiest men in the land," continued the captain.

The bishop, his vanity poked and his interest piqued, asked if there might be time for him to visit the hermits. Since the winds and weather had been so favorable, the captain indicated that they would have no problem stopping for a visit and still making their scheduled appointment in Rome.

Soon the bishop, dressed in his splendid robes and surrounded by his advisors, boarded a rowboat that carried them off to the little island. As soon as the bishop stepped on the sand, the three hermits prostrated themselves in front of him. After blessing them the bishop asked, "What do you spend all of your time doing here in this desolate place?"

"We spend our time seeking to better love God," responded one of the hermits hesitantly.

"And what are you studying?" queried the bishop.

The puzzled hermits looked at each other and did not respond.

"Simpletons," thought the bishop, and he decided to waste no more time with the hermits.

(continued)

"Let us say the Lord's Prayer, and then I will be off," said the bishop with a yawn. Again the hermits looked at each other in bewilderment.

"You mean you do not know the Lord's Prayer?" the bishop cried in amazement.

The hermits shook their heads no.

"Then how can you seek him?" he muttered.

The hermits lowered their heads apologetically and said, "Oh sir, if it would help us to love God more, we would be pleased to learn."

The bishop, with an air of patronage, replied dryly, "At least I can teach you this," and he begin to recite the Lord's Prayer. He then encouraged the hermits to repeat it after him.

They were very slow learners. For several exasperating hours the bishop sat with the hermits, going over and over the words until each could haltingly make their way through the exercise.

The bishop quickly said a prayer over the three hermits and tumbled back into the rowboat. The entourage made their way wearily back to the ship.

"Well?" the captain asked.

"Sheer idiots, mindless morons, a waste of my time," spat out the bishop. "Let's get under the wind!"

As the crew raised the anchor, one of the sailors cried out for the captain. "Ahoy! Men off the starboard bow," he shouted.

It was the three hermits, and to the astonishment of everyone on board, they were walking towards the ship on the water!

Once on board they bowed low before the bishop, and with heads hung low one of them said, "Your excellency, we desire for you to teach us how to love our Savior more, but we are ashamed to say we have forgotten the last line of the prayer you taught us."

Then the bishop, humbled to his core, got down on his knees in front of the three hermits and said, "My brothers, you have no need of me to teach you anything. Give me your blessing and I will go in peace."

Where to take it from here...

True spirituality comes not from how much you know about God but from how much you love God. "Knowledge puffs up, but love builds up. The man who thinks he knows something does not yet know as he ought to know. But the man who loves God is known by God" (1 Corinthians 8:1-3).

The Scar Study

A scientific researcher gathered 10 volunteers for a special psychological study called the Scar Experiment. Separating the volunteers into 10 different cubicles without mirrors, she explained that the purpose of the study was to examine how other people would respond to a stranger with a physical deformity, such as a facial scar.

Using makeup tricks straight out of Hollywood, the scientist put bloody and gruesome scars on each volunteer's left cheek. She showed each volunteer the new "scar" with a small hand-held mirror and then put the mirror away.

The researcher's final step in each cubicle was to tell each volunteer that she needed to put some finishing powder on his or her scar to prevent it from smearing. In reality, she used a tissue to wipe off the scar. The volunteers, however, believed they still had scars on their faces. Each volunteer was then sent out into the waiting rooms of different medical offices with instructions to notice how strangers in the office responded to the scar.

After the appointed time, all 10 volunteers returned with the same report. They noticed that strangers were more rude to them, less kind to them, and stared at their "scar."

Where to take it from here...

Preoccupied with our personal flaws (physical or otherwise), we often assume that other people consider our flaws as repulsive as we do. In reality, most people hardly notice the things we thing are wrong with us. Because our flaws consume us, we may act toward others as if they disapproved of us. That makes it hard to form friendships.

On the other hand, having a healthy self-image or taking a positive view of ourselves frees us to enjoy healthier relationships.

Ultimately, of course, a healthy self-image comes from knowing that God thinks highly of you. He created you and loves you as his child. When you take time to listen to God's voice telling you who you really are, you will be less likely to worry about what others think of you.

I DIDN'T KNOW THAT!

- *Stewardesses* is the longest word that can be typed with only the left hand.
- An ostrich's eye is bigger than its brain.
- White Out was invented by the mother of the Monkee's Michael Nesmith.
- A pregnant goldfish is called a *twit.*
- In England the Speaker of the House is not allowed to speak.
- To escape the grip of a crocodile's jaws, push your thumbs into its eyeballs. It will let you go instantly.
- Frank Sinatra never owned a pair of Levis.
- If a cat falls off the seventh floor of a building, it has about 30 percent less chance of surviving than a cat falling off the twentieth floor. It takes about eight floors for a cat to realize what is happening, relax, and correct itself.
- Look at your zipper. See the initials YKK? It stands for Yoshida Kogyo Kabushibibaisha, the world's largest zipper manufacturer.
- The Monongahela River's name translated into English means "high banks breaking off and falling down in places."
- A mathematical wonder: 111,111,111 multiplied by 111,111,111 gives the result 12,345,678,987,654,321.
- No word in the English language rhymes with month, orange, silver, and purple.
- Canada is an Indian word meaning "Big Village."
- "I am" is the shortest complete sentence in the English language.
- The term "the whole 9 yards" came from WWII fighter pilots in the South Pacific. The ammo belts for .50 caliber machine guns measured exactly 27 feet before being loaded into the fuselage. If the pilots fired all their ammo at a target, it got "the whole 9 yards."
- The most common name in the world is Mohammed.
- Mel Blanc (the voice of Bugs Bunny) was allergic to carrots.
- The very first bomb dropped by the Allies on Berlin during World War II killed the only elephant in the Berlin Zoo.

- A "jiffy" is the name for an actual unit of time—1/100th of a second.
- The average person falls asleep in seven minutes.
- Hershey's Kisses are called that because the machine that makes them looks like it's kissing the conveyor belt.
- The phrase "rule of thumb" is derived from an old English law which stated that you couldn't beat your wife with anything wider than your thumb.
- The longest recorded flight of a chicken is 13 seconds.
- The "pound" (#) key on your keyboard is called an octothorp.
- The only domestic animal not mentioned in the Bible is the cat.
- The "dot" over the letter "i" is called a tittle.
- Honey is the only natural food that is made without destroying any kind of life. What about milk you say? A cow has to eat grass to produce milk and grass is living.
- Winston Churchill was born in a ladies' room during a dance.
- Dr. Seuss pronounced "Seuss" such that it rhymed with "rejoice."
- More people are killed annually by donkeys than die in air crashes.
- Armored knights raised their visors to identify themselves when they rode past their king. That's how we got the modern military salute.
- Los Angeles's full name is: "El Pueblo de Nuestra Senora la Reina de los Angeles de Poriuncula."
- Tigers have striped skin, not just striped fur.
- Hummingbirds are the only animal that can fly backwards.
- A cat's jaw cannot move sideways.

Where to take it from here...

Although these pieces of "useless trivia" are true, none of them require any action or response on our part. And knowing them won't improve the quality of your life—or anyone else's for that matter.

But there's a kind of truth that can change your life! That truth is the Word of God. Jesus promised that you could know the truth, "and the truth shall set you free." The writer of Hebrews described the Word of God as quick and powerful and sharper than a two-edged sword (4:12).

If you think that the Bible is nothing more than ancient trivia, think again! It has the power to do a mighty work in your life. That's why Christians want to spend time in God's Word every day, even though they may already know what's in the Bible. You need to allow the Bible to do its work on you. God speaks to us and changes us through his Word. Read it and you will experience true freedom in Christ!

The Mystery of the Mop

Everyone at the State University knew that Donner Hall had the best parties. All-night dancing and beer guzzling attracted the largest weekend crowds by far—especially on the notorious second floor. By midnight every Friday and Saturday, the entire second floor was three inches deep in smashed beer cans, empty wine bottles, and stale potato chips.

But by about 7:00 a.m. the next morning, all of the garbage was removed. The second floor residents assumed the conscientious school janitors came bright and early, before anyone woke up, to sweep up the mess.

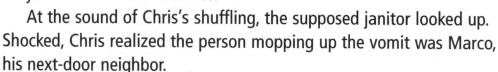

Early one Saturday morning, Chris, still hung over from Friday night's party, stumbled out of his bed to head for the bathroom. Noticing a freshly vacuumed second floor, he mumbled to himself, "I guess the janitors came early again to get rid of the mess."

On reaching the bathroom, however, his nose warned him the mess wasn't completely eliminated. A trail of vomit soiled the bathroom floor, ending at the point where someone was just then mopping it up. Chris thought to himself, I'm glad the janitor is doing the dirty work so we don't have to.

At the sound of Chris's shuffling, the supposed janitor looked up. Shocked, Chris realized the person mopping up the vomit was Marco, his next-door neighbor.

"Marco, man, what are you doing?" Chris asked.

Marco answered simply, "I'm cleaning up."

"Why? You weren't even at the party last night."

"Because I'm a Christian."

No janitor had ever cared enough to clean up every Monday morning. It had been Marco the whole time.

Where to take it from here...

Marco's model of servant leadership is required of all who follow of Jesus. In what ways have you shown yourself to be willing to serve others—to do what Jesus would do, even if nobody knows it's you doing it?

In the Dark

A young soldier and his commanding officer got on a train together. The only available seats were across from an attractive young lady who was traveling with her grandmother. As the four engaged in conversation, the soldier and the young lady kept eyeing one another. There was an obvious mutual attraction.

Suddenly the train went into a tunnel, sending the train car into darkness. Immediately two sounds were heard: the smack of a kiss followed by the whack of a slap across someone's face.

The grandmother thought, I can't believe he kissed my granddaughter, but I'm glad she gave him the slap he deserved.

The commanding officer thought, I don't blame the boy for kissing the girl, but it's a shame that she missed him and hit me instead.

The young girl thought, I'm glad he kissed me, but I wish my grandmother hadn't slapped him for doing it.

And as the train broke into the sunlight, the soldier couldn't help but smile. He had managed to kiss a pretty girl and slap his commanding officer and get away with both!

Where to take it from here...

It's hard to get away with anything in the light. That's why so many people love the darkness (John 3:19).

The Golden Fish

Children in Bosnia-Herzegovina all know the ancient story of the poor woman who caught a golden fish, released it, and in return gained wealth and happiness. According to a 1998 Associated Press story, this Balkan fairy tale turned into reality for one poor family.

Before the start of the Bosnian war, the Malkoc family lived next to a small lake in the northwestern village of Jezero. One day in 1990, Smajo Malkoc returned from a trip to Austria with an unusual gift for his teenage sons, Dzevad and Catib: an aquarium with two goldfish.

Two years passed before Bosnian Serb forces advanced on Jezero. The women and children fled, and the men stayed back to resist the attacking soldiers. Smajo Malkoc was killed. When his wife, Fehima, sneaked back into the destroyed village to bury her husband and rescue what remained of their belongings, she took pity on the fish in the aquarium. She let them out into the nearby lake, saying to herself, "This way, they might be more fortunate than us."

Fast-forward to 1995. Fehima Malkoc returned with her sons to Jezero. Nothing but ruins remained of their home and their village. Through misty eyes she looked toward the lake. Glimpsing something strange, she walked over to the shore.

"The whole lake was shining from the thousands of golden fish in it," she said. "It made me immediately think of my husband. This was something he left me that I never hoped for."

During the years of killing all around the lake, life underwater had flourished. After their return, Fehima Malkoc and her sons started caring for and selling the goldfish.

By 1998, homes, stores, and coffee shops all over the region feature aquariums containing fish from Jezero. The Malkoc house, rebuilt on its original site, is one of the biggest in the village. Two new cars are parked in front, and the family says it has enough money to quit worrying about the future.

"It was a special kind of gift from our father," Dzevad Malkoc said.

(continued)

Where to take it from here...

One can never underestimate what a gift of love or an act of kindness might produce. Jesus said, "Give, and it will be given to you" (Luke 6:38). Whenever you give, no matter how small and insignificant your gift might be, God blesses it and uses it to accomplish great things. Jesus took a young boy's lunch and fed a multitude. Have no doubt that he can take whatever we offer to him and turn it into something magnificent.

The Malkoc's story is also a parable of God's relentless grace at work even in the midst of chaos and trouble. While the war in Bosnia was raging, life below the surface of a small lake flourished. We can rest assured that God's will is being done—that his kingdom is flourishing—even when life on the surface is full of trouble and strife. That is the message of the gospel—the ultimate fairy tale that comes true.

Shut Up and Fish

Old Pete had a knack for catching fish. Every weekend Old Pete went fishing and returned with dozens of fish. Nobody knew how he did it. When other fisherman were unable to land more than three or four, Old Pete always came back with stringer after stringer of freshly caught fish.

Curious, the fish and game warden decided to investigate. He followed Old Pete out to the lake, and when he launched his boat at the dock, the warden asked if he could ride along and observe.

"Sure," said Old Pete. "Hop in."

Old Pete started up his outboard motor. When they arrived at an obscure reach of the lake, Pete stopped the boat. The warden sat back and watched.

Reaching into a box, Pete pulled out a stick of dynamite, lit it, and tossed it into the water. After the explosion dead fish soon started rising to the surface. Old Pete took out a net and started scooping them up.

"Wait a minute!" said the warden. "What do you think you're doing? You can't do that! I'll put you in jail, buddy! You'll be paying every fine in the book! You'll never fish again!"

Old Pete calmly put down his net, picked up a second stick of dynamite, lit it, and tossed it in the warden's lap.

"So are you gonna sit there criticizing me all day," he asked the panicked warden, "or are you gonna fish?"

Where to take it from here...

The fish and game warden was quickly transformed from passive observer to, shall we say, enthusiastic participant. It's always easy to criticize other people from a distance, but what will you do when you find yourself in a similar situation? Decisions aren't nearly as neat and clear when you're the one in a tough place.

Too Polite

Hannah Whitall Smith tells the story of the man who was walking along a road, carrying a heavy burden on his shoulders. A wagon overtook him and the driver kindly offered to give the man a ride. The man happily accepted the offer, but even when he was seated on the wagon, he continued to carry the heavy load on his shoulders.

Perplexed, the kindhearted wagon driver said, "Sir, why don't you put down your burden? There's plenty of room."

"Oh, no," said the man. "I feel it's almost too much to ask you to carry *me.* I wouldn't think of asking you to carry my burden also."

Where to take it from here...

Maybe you are like that man. You've allowed Christ to carry you—to be your Savior—but you are unwilling to entrust certain areas of your life to his care. Jesus wants control of your whole life: "Come to me, all you who are weary and burdened, and I will give you rest" (Matthew 11:28). If there are problems in your life too heavy for you to bear alone, give them to Jesus. He will carry your load.

THE COACH

Bud Wilkinson's football teams at the University of Oklahoma were undoubtedly the strongest in the nation in the late 50s and early 60s. Consistently his undefeated teams steamrolled the opposition. After his retirement to the broadcast booth, Coach Wilkinson was asked the secret of his success. How could he consistently mold young athletes into powerful teams, year after year?

This was Bud's answer:

"When a football player goes into a game, he can play to a variety of audiences. He may play for the crowd in the stands, for example, working hard for their cheers and avoiding their boos. Or he might play for a special person in the stands—a girlfriend, maybe.

"A player may allow the other team to dictate his play. In other words, if the man across the line isn't very good, then he doesn't play well either. If the opponent cheats and plays dirty, so does he.

"Some football players allow their teammates to determine the quality of their play. Some focus on the game officials, the referees. And of course, some play merely for themselves—they work hard to be the stars.

"Many audiences vie for the attention of the players. My men know, however, that there's only one person watching the game that matters—only one person whom they have to please...me. Regardless of the cheers or boos, the strength of the opposition, the fairness of the officials, or the play of their teammates, I am the only audience that counts. When everyone knows that and plays that way, they pull together, do their best, give it their all, and win."

Where to take it from here...

Christians sometimes play to the crowd, to our peers, or to any of a number of audiences. But only one person in the stands really counts—God. We need to play our lives for him and him alone (Philippians 3:13-14; Hebrews 12:2).

The Man Who Changed the World

Once upon a time a man set out to change the world. Before long he discovered that the world was far too big for one person to change. So he decided to change his country.

Crooked politicians and special interest groups unfortunately thwarted his efforts, so he decided to change his neighborhood. But his neighbors simply closed their doors and shut their windows, so he decided to change his family. Instead of changing, his children rebelled and his wife threatened a divorce, and things only got worse.

Finally, the man decided to change himself.

And when he did that, he changed the world.

Where to take it from here...

Change starts with you.

The High Dive

Charley and Matt lived in a nice neighborhood where the people were friendly—except for one man who lived at the end of the street in a big house with a gigantic swimming pool. His pool had the highest diving board they had ever seen—so high they could see it over the big fence that surrounded his property.

Every day Charley and Matt walked past the man's house wishing they could dive off that diving board. But the man didn't allow anyone on his property, especially kids. The *No Trespassing* sign made that very clear, but the prohibition only made the boys want to get inside all the more. They made a pact with each other that the next time their neighbor went out of town they would sneak over the fence late at night and dive off his incredible high dive.

Two weeks later they noticed the man load a couple of suitcases in his trunk. Peeking through the blinds in Matt's bedroom, they saw him drive away. Charley and Matt felt a rush. They knew that tonight they'd get to experience the thrill they had been dreaming about.

Around 11:00 p.m., dressed in their swimsuits and wrapped in their towels, they snuck out of their bedrooms to meet at the old man's house. Although it was a moonless night, they didn't use flashlights in case someone might see them. They definitely didn't want their parents finding out.

Climbing over the fence, they entered the man's yard. Even in the pitch-dark night they could make out the form of a second fence right next to the pool—which they immediately climbed over.

Inside the pool area they couldn't see a thing. Charley was feeling his way along, looking for a place to put his towel, when Matt bumped into the diving board. He immediately started climbing to the top of the ladder. "Last one in is a rotten egg!" he called to Charley, laughing.

"Be quiet!" Charley said as he felt his way to the edge of the pool. He wanted to check the temperature of the water. He sat down on the edge and tried to lower his foot in the water when he heard Matt spring

off the board. And just about the time Charley made his discovery, he heard a thud and a bloodcurdling scream.

What Charley discovered was that there was no water in the pool. The old man had drained it. Matt hit the bottom of the pool feet first and suffered a broken back and other serious injuries which left him paralyzed the rest of his life.

Where to take it from here...

Charley and Matt chose to ignore the fences that the owner had put up to protect people from the danger on the other side. God puts up a different kind of fence to protect us from getting hurt, physically or spiritually. When we choose to ignore God's fences—whether it's in the area of sex, drugs, drinking, honesty, etc.—we will experience consequences that could seriously hurt us.

TOSSING THE QUEEN

During the heyday of the Napoleonic era, French troops fanned out around the globe to share the "best" of France with their colonies and to bring the best things from those colonies back to France.

Included in this "cultural exchange" was a storehouse filled with ancient Egyptian artifacts. As the empire waned, many of these treasures found their way into the basement of the Paris museum.

In the 1940s some workmen uncovered a burial case squeezed into an obscure corner of the basement. They decided that the box would make an excellent storage space for many of the treasures. Without consulting the museum's caretakers, they simply emptied the contents into the sewer and filled it with odds and ends of Egyptian artifacts.

Only later did they discover that they had inadvertently disposed of the remains of Egypt's most famous personage—Cleopatra.

Where to take it from here...

In ignorance people regularly discard things of great value. Jesus Christ is God's greatest gift to mankind, yet he continues to be rejected by "those who do not believe" (1 Peter 2:7).

A Meeting with the Top Dog

The president of the Doggie Vittles dog food company summoned his managers to an emergency meeting in his office.

Pacing the room, he barked out a series of questions.

"Men and women, my fellow employees! Tell me! *What dog food company has the most nutritious dog food in all of America?*"

The managers all shouted back, "Doggie Vittles, sir!"

"And *what dog food company has the most attractive packaging of any dog food company in America?*"

"Doggie Vittles, sir!" they replied in unison.

"And *what dog food company has spent more on advertising than any other dog food company in America?*"

"Doggie Vittles, sir!" they yelled back.

The president paused before shouting out a last question. "Then *why—why aren't we selling more dog food than any other dog food company in America?*"

The room went very quiet. Finally, someone in the back of the room spoke up.

"Well, sir, it's because *the dogs don't like it.*"

Where to take it from here...

Big events, big names, high-tech programming, and fun activities often attract new kids to our youth group. But all the flash must be backed by our friendship and love and by our message of the good news about Jesus Christ. It doesn't matter how much money we spend or how many exciting attractions we present, unless kids have their social and spiritual needs met, they won't keep coming back.

Jimmy's Ranch

When Jimmy was a little boy, he wanted to be a cowboy. He spent countless hours in front of the television, watching reruns of *Gunsmoke* and *Bonanza*. He just knew that someday he would live on a ranch, wear a big cowboy hat, and ride the range just like all his cowboy heroes. When he was seven years old, Jimmy said, "Dad, I want to be a cowboy when I grow up. Will you help me be a cowboy?"

"Sure, son," said his dad, smiling down on his little cowpoke. As the years went by, Jimmy grew into a fine young man. As you might expect, he outgrew his childhood fantasy of becoming a cowboy and turned instead to girls, sports, studying, and preparing himself for a career in the business world.

One day Jimmy went to his father again and said, "Dad, I want to go to college and get a good education. Will you help me?"

His dad said, "College? Son, you can't go to college. When you were seven, you said you wanted to be a cowboy. So I bought you a ranch in Texas with 50 head of cattle! There's no money for you to go to college. Besides, you need to take care of that ranch. It's all yours."

"But Dad!" said Jimmy. "I was just a child when I said that! I didn't know then what I know now! I don't want a ranch! I want an education!"

Where to take it from here...

Have you ever wondered why God doesn't answer your prayers exactly the way you want him to? Maybe it's because we're like Jimmy. As God's children, we don't always know what's best for us.

Instead of grumbling about "unanswered" prayers, we should be thankful God doesn't always answer our prayers the way we think he should. If he did, we might end up like Jimmy—with a ranch instead of an education. God knows exactly what you need, even when you don't. In fact, the Bible teaches that when you pray, the Holy Spirit actually prays for you, too (Romans 8:26-28). Because of this, we can relax and know that whatever happens will be according to God's will.

A Purifying Fire

Violent winds drove a devastating fire through Yellowstone National Park a few years back. Hot, dry weather mocked heroic fire fighters who battled day and night trying to save lives, buildings, and precious landscapes. In spite of their efforts, this monster fire scorched thousands of acres. When the smoke cleared, blackened and starkly bare hills had replaced the beautifully forested wilderness.

A few months after the fire, a national park forest ranger escorting a group of tourists through the park shocked them by saying, "Apart from the structures burned and the lives that were endangered, this fire was the very best thing that could have happened to this park."

He explained the need for the choking underbrush to be totally cleared out. "Then from the ashes," he continued, "come wonderful nutrients for the soil. New life is now allowed to spring forth. The future of Yellowstone forest land depends upon purifying fires every 50 years or so. What we viewed as tragedy was nature's way of preserving and protecting the future. You won't believe how beautiful this park will be in about 10 years."

Where to take it from here...

Personal losses or family tragedies or changes in relationships are like purifying fires in our lives. When our personal monster fire is raging, or when it smolders in the middle of what seems to be a disaster, all we can see is the ashes and the pain. Often, however, those fires make new life possible for us. Sometimes things have to die before growth can take place (John 12:24).

Why 1 Never Eat

Everybody has a good excuse for not attending church. If you take those excuses and apply them to other things we do (or don't do), like eating, they might look like this list:

I don't eat any more because…
1. I was forced to eat as a child.
2. People who eat all the time are hypocrites; they aren't really hungry.
3. There are so many different kinds of food, I can't decide what to eat.
4. I used to eat, but I got bored and stopped.
5. I only eat on special occasions, like Christmas and Easter.
6. None of my friends will eat with me.
7. I'll start eating when I get older.
8. I don't really have time to eat.
9. I don't believe that eating does anybody any good. It's just a crutch.
10. Restaurants and grocery stores are only after your money.

Where to take it from here...

Giving a lame excuse for not attending church or for not getting involved in ministry is just as silly as giving up eating. Church attendance for the Christian is as important as regular, balanced meals. Without spiritual food, we will die. (1 Peter 2:2).

THE FARMER'S THREE WISHES

An ancient Jewish parable:

One night a poor farmer was awakened by an angel of the Lord who said: "You've found favor in the eyes of your Maker. He wants to do for you what he did for your ancestor Abraham. He wants to bless you. Therefore, make any three requests of God, and he will be pleased to give them to you. There's only one condition: your neighbor will get a double portion of everything that is given to you."

The farmer was so startled by all this that he woke up his wife and told her all about it. She insisted they put it to the test. So they prayed, "Oh, blessed God, if we could just have a herd of a thousand cattle, that would enable us to break out of the poverty in which we've lived for generations. That would be wonderful."

No sooner had they said these words than they heard the sound of animal noises outside. Lo and behold, all around the house were a thousand magnificent cattle! During the next two days, the farmer's feet hardly touched the ground. He divided his time between praising God for his great generosity and making practical provisions for his newly found affluence.

On the third afternoon he was up on a hill behind his house, trying to decide where to build a new barn when, for the first time, he looked across at his neighbor's field, and there on the green hillside stood two thousand magnificent cattle. For the first time since the angel of the Lord had appeared, his joy evaporated and a scowl of envy took its place. He went home that evening in a foul mood, refused to eat supper, and went to bed in an absolute rage. He couldn't fall asleep, because every time he closed his eyes, all he could see were his neighbor's two thousand head of cattle.

Deep in the night, however, he remembered that the angel had said he could make three wishes. With that he shifted his focus away from his neighbor and back to his own situation, and the old joy quickly returned. Digging into his own heart to find out what else he really wanted, he began to realize that in addition to some kind of material security, he had always wanted descendants to carry on his name into history. So he prayed a second time saying, "Gracious God, if it please thee, give me a child that I may have descendants." It wasn't long before his wife came to him with the news that she was bearing in her body a life not her own.

The next months were passed in unbroken joy. The farmer was busy with his newly acquired affluence and looking forward to the great grace of becoming a parent. On the night his first child was born, he was absolutely overjoyed. The next day was the Sabbath. He went to the synagogue and at the time of the prayers of the people, he stood up and shared with the gathered community his great good fortune: now at last a child had been born into their home!

He had hardly sat down, however, when his neighbor got up. "God has indeed been gracious to our little community. I had twin sons born last night. Thanks be to God." On hearing that, the farmer went home in an utterly different mood from the one in which he came. Instead of being joyful, he was filled with the canker of jealousy.

This time, the dark emotions didn't go away. Late that evening, he made his third request of God, which was, "Lord, please gouge out my right eye."

No sooner had he said these words than the angel who started the whole process came again. "Why, son of Abraham, have your turned to such dark desirings?"

With pent-up rage, the farmer replied, "I can't stand to see my neighbor prosper! I'll gladly sacrifice half my vision for the satisfaction of knowing that he'll never be able to look on what he has."

Those words were followed by a long silence, and as the farmer looked, he saw tears forming in the eyes of the angel.

"Why, O son of Abraham, have you turned the occasion to bless into a time of hurting? Your third request won't be granted, not because the Lord lacks integrity, but because he is full of mercy. However, know this, O foolish one, you've brought sadness, not only to yourself, but to the very heart of God."

(continued)

The moral of this story? If you want to be miserable, then compare what you have with what other people have. There will always be somebody with more than you, and they will always be (in your opinion, anyway) less deserving.

Jesus told a similar story in Matthew 20:1-16 about a vineyard owner and a few workers who grew resentful of those who had received equal pay for less work. Rather than being grateful for the good pay they had been promised and had received, they were unhappy and critical of the vineyard owner for not giving them more.

That's why one of the Ten Commandments is "Thou shalt not covet" (Exodus 20:17). To covet, to be jealous of what other people have, to envy those who have more—these negative emotions rob you of your happiness and keep you from praising God for what he has given to you. If you compare yourself to those who have less, you may become proud; if you compare yourself to those who have more, you will probably become resentful. God wants you to be content and grateful regardless of what you have (Philippians 4:11-12). Only then can he give you more.

MoNKey Addicts

A scientist conducted an experiment in which he made cocaine available to some monkeys. These monkeys could pull a lever in their cages to release a little cocaine into their feeding tray. Not surprisingly, the monkeys became addicted to the drug. As the experiment continued, the scientist found that if the addicted monkeys could get additional cocaine hits any time they wanted by just pulling the lever, all of them would overdose. They all ended up killing themselves.

The scientist then tried another experiment with addicted monkeys. He began to withhold the fix when the monkey pulled the lever. Over and over these monkeys pulled the lever, trying to get cocaine. They continued to pull the lever not ten times, not a hundred times, or even a thousand times. Those addicted monkeys pulled it an average of 12,800 times!

Where to take it from here...

Powerful addictions can rule the lives of people—addictions to work, food, gambling, sex, alcohol, or drugs. Some finally reach a point where they lose any hope of breaking free. Some even turn aside from help offered, convinced that they're a hopeless case.

But there's hope in Christ. He can set any person free from the addiction of sin. He can give you a fresh start on your life. When you invite Christ into your life, the change begins to take place—from the inside out. You can't beat addictions on your own, but through the power of Christ, you can be set free. "I no longer live, but Christ lives in me" (Galatians 2:20).

An Idiot's Guide to Easter

On Easter Sunday Little Johnny listened as his Sunday school teacher told the class that the lesson would be about the meaning of Easter. "Can anyone tell the Easter story?" she asked. When no one volunteered to speak, she called on Frank.

"Umm, I don't think I know," Frank said. The teacher reassured him that was okay and moved on to Betty.

"I don't know how to tell it," she responded.

Finally, Little Johnny decided to raise his hand. He said he would tell the Easter story. The teacher was pleasantly surprised at his willingness, since he was usually the class clown.

"On Easter," said Johnny, "Jesus and his disciples were eating the Jewish Passover at the last supper, but later Jesus was deceived and turned over to the Romans by one of his disciples. He was accused of teaching he was the Messiah and when he confessed it, the Romans made him wear a crown of thorns, took him to be crucified, and hung him on a cross with nails through his hands and feet. He said 'It is

——————— *Still More* Hot Illustrations for Youth Talks

finished' which means 'Debt paid in full' and died. He was definitely dead because the water was separated from his blood when they stabbed his side. So they buried him in a nearby cave on Friday which was sealed off by a large boulder."

"Very good, Johnny! the teacher gasped excitedly. "And what else happened that we celebrate on Easter?"

Johnny thought for a moment before continuing. "Now, on Easter Sunday each year, we move the boulder aside so that Jesus can come out. And if he sees his shadow, then we know there will be six more weeks of winter!"

Where to take it from here...

How would you tell the Easter Story? According to Scripture, the resurrection of Christ is the centerpiece of our faith. There are many people who believe in Jesus—who believe that he died on the cross for our sins—but who have a hard time believing in the Resurrection. Paul clearly teaches that without a risen Christ, we have no gospel at all. Unless you believe in the risen Christ, our religion is pointless. But because he was raised from the dead, we will also be raised to eternal life. Now that's good news! (1 Corinthians 15:13-14).

The New Irrational Version [NIV]

This collection of comments about the Bible was actually written by children.

The Bible is full of interesting caricatures. In the first book of the Bible, Guinessis, God got tired of creating the world, so he took the Sabbath off. Adam and Eve were created from an apple tree. One of their children, Cain, asked "Am I my brother's son?"

Noah's wife was called Joan of Ark. Noah built an ark, which the animals came to in pears. Lot's wife was a pillar of salt by day, but a ball of fire by night. God asked Abraham to sacrifice Isaac on Mount Montezuma. Jacob, son of Isaac, stole his brother's birthmark. Jacob was a partridge who had twelve sons. One of Jacob's sons, Joseph, gave refuse to the Israelites.

Sampson was a strong man who let himself be led astray by Jezebel. Then he slayed the Philistines with the ax of the apostles.

People who lived in Egypt were called mummies. They lived in the Sarah Dessert and traveled by Camelot. The climate of the Sarah is so hot that it is cultivated by irritation. The Egyptians built the Pyramids in the shape of a huge triangular cube. The Pyramids are a range of mountains between France and Spain.

Pharaoh forced the Hebrew slaves to make bread without straw. Moses led the Hebrews to the Red Sea, where they made unleavened bread, which is bread without any ingredients. The Egyptians were all drowned in the dessert. Afterward, Moses went up to Mount Cyanide to get the Ten Amendments. The First Commandment was when Eve told Adam to eat the apple. The Fifth Commandment is humor thy father and mother. The Seventh Commandment is thou shalt not admit adultery.

Moses died before he ever reached Canada. Then Joshua led the Hebrews in the battle to Geritol. The greatest miracle in the Bible is when Joshua told his son to stand still and he obeyed him.

David was a Hebrew king skilled at playing the liar. He fought with the Finkelsteins, a race of people who lived in Biblical times. Solomon, one of David's sons, had 300 wives and 700 porcupines.

When Mary heard that she was the Mother of Jesus, she sang the Magna Carta. When the three wise guys from the east side arrived, they found Jesus in the Manager. Jesus was born because Mary had an immaculate contraption. St. John, the Blacksmith, dumped water on his head.

Jesus said the Golden Rule, which says to do one to others before they do one to you. He also explained, "Man doth not live by sweat alone."

The people who followed the Lord were called the twelve decibels. The epistles were the wives of apostles. One of the opossums was St. Matthew, who was by profession a taxi man. St. Paul cavorted to Christianity. He preached holy acrimony, which is another name for marriage. A Christian should have only one wife. This is called monotony.

(continued)

Where to take it from here...

Unfortunately, children are not the only ones who misinterpret or misunderstand the Bible. Adults, too, are often Biblically illiterate. That's why it's important to read the Bible for yourself and to attend Bible studies and classes that will help you to learn what the Bible really says and means. The Bible is God's love letter to you. It is full of wonderful stories and teachings that are not only very interesting, but they will help you to live a happier, more successful life.

THE BABY WILDEBEEST

Wildebeests, a type of African antelope also known as gnus, migrate yearly in huge herds to the plains of Tanzania's Serengeti to mate and to birth their young. Also on the Serengeti Plain roam vicious predators, including the hyena. In this hostile setting a newborn wildebeest has about 15 minutes to get up and run with the adult herd. Slow starters risk becoming hyena lunch.

Discovery Channel showed film of a wildebeest giving birth on the Serengeti. Her baby barely had time to get used to breathing when the mother nudged it to get it standing. Picture the newborn on wobbly hind legs with its forelegs still bent underneath its bobbing head. Between the mother's nudging and the baby's inexperience, the newborn is worn out after five minutes of repeated attempts to stand.

Then the camera picks up a hyena approaching stiff-legged with low-ered head and slightly bared teeth. The mother wildebeest bravely steps between the hyena and the baby, but another hyena appears, followed closely by a third. The mother lunges at the newcomer. Although it backs away, another skulks in closer to the helpless infant. Before long a circle of hyenas occupies the mother wildebeest while other hyenas eat the baby.

Meanwhile, spread out nearby, literally thousands of other wildebeest graze, now and then lifting their heads to watch the desperate mother attempt to fight off the hyenas. Any of them could easily help save the newborn, but not a single one does.

Where to take it from here...

Satan, like the hyena, is on the prowl. He also has lots of help. If you try to stand up to him alone, you're almost guaranteed defeat—just like that mother wildebeest.

You can't survive spiritually without other Christians who support you, encourage you, pray for you, and help you grow into a strong follower of

Jesus Christ. That's why, when you become a Christian, you are adopted into the family of God (Ephesians 1:5). That's why God created the church.

Our habit in today's world is to live our lives alone. To stay out of each other's affairs. To keep our distance. That's not God's way, though. He asks us to love each other and to care for each other, as brothers and sisters in Christ. We weren't made to be like all those wildebeest in the herd that stood off to the side watching one of their own get eaten alive by hyenas.

Little Rivets, Big Disaster

Over 1,500 people died in the worst maritime disaster of all time—the sinking of the *Titanic* on its maiden voyage from England to New York. On an April night in 1912, the luxurious 900-foot-long cruise ship hit an iceberg and sank. At least that's what historians believe, as well as the script writers of the hit movie.

An international team of divers and scientists has challenged that theory. Using sound waves to probe through the wreckage lying in mud some two and a half miles below the surface, they discovered that the damage was surprisingly small. Instead of a huge gash, they found six relatively narrow slits across six watertight holds.

Further, a salvage team recovered several of the rivets which secured the damaged hull. Analysis revealed the rivets were made of a low-grade steel. This has led scientists to propose that the *Titanic* sank not because of a collision with the iceberg, but because of a few small rivets of inferior quality. Had these rivets held, the ship may have survived the impact of the collision.

Where to take it from here...

The failure of a tiny rivet can sink a colossal ship.
We, too, can be sunk by small sins, small omissions, small compromises. Failures in the areas of our lives that may be invisible to others have a way of doing visible damage.

No Greater Love

In the open salvos of World War II, a large British military force on the European continent, as well as English citizens and diplomats, retreated to the French coastal port of Dunkirk. With its back against the English Channel, the British army faced a German army that threatened to drive it into the sea. To save what he could of his army, British prime minister Winston Churchill called for all available sea vessels, whether large or small, to evacuate the soldiers and civilians from the besieged French beaches and bring them back across the Channel to safety.

An incredible array of ships and boats raced to the rescue—fishing boats and cruise ships alike. As the flotilla made its way to the beach to pick up soldiers and then move out again, Nazi aircraft set upon them like vultures while German artillery pummeled them with shells. Ships were strafed with machine gun fire, and some were blown out of the water altogether.

Three German Messerschmits attacked the defenseless *Lancastria,* a converted cruise liner whose decks and hold were packed with soldiers. One bomb dropped directly down the ship's smokestack, tearing a huge gap in her lower hull. Nearly 200 men were trapped in the forward hold of the now severely listing ship. No one doubted that the liner was going down. Chaos, smoke, oil, fire, and blood, mixed with terrified cries of the men trapped below, created pandemonium on deck as those hopeful of surviving searched for lifeboats or simply leaped into the water.

Moving through the middle of this living nightmare, a young Navy chaplain quietly worked his way to the edge of the hold and peered in at the darkness below.

Then, knowing he could never get out, he dropped into the hole.

Survivors later told how the only thing that gave them courage to survive until passing ships could rescue them was hearing the strong, brave voices of the men in the hold singing hymns as the ship finally rolled over and went to the bottom.

This true story testifies to the courage and compassion of one faithful Christian who gave his life to provide comfort, courage, and hope to the suffering. We are also called to demonstrate that kind of love in our lost and dying world. "Greater love has no one than this..." (John 15:13).

YOU CALL THIS A SERVICE STATION?

One day a lady pulled into a self-serve gas station to fill up her car. She got out of her car, hurried over to the pump, lifted the nozzle to her gas tank, and tried to pump the gas. Nothing happened. Belatedly she realized that this was one of those gas stations where you had to prepay. Frustrated and in a hurry, she ran inside, paid the cashier, and returned to her car to resume pumping her gas.

She squeezed the handle, but still nothing happened. "What kind of lousy gas station is this?" she mumbled angrily to herself. After trying again with no better results, she ran back in to the cashier and started giving him a piece of her mind. With a concerned look on his face, the cashier talked right over the top of the lady's scolding

"Ma'am, please stay right here. Don't go back to your car. I just called 911. When you were leaving the building after paying me, I saw a man get into the back seat of your car. It looked to me like he didn't belong there. The only way I could get you to come back inside was to turn off your gas pump."

Just then the police pulled up and took into custody the man who was hiding in the woman's car. The woman learned later that he was trying to get initiated into a very dangerous gang. Armed with a knife, he had planned to kill her and steal her car once they left the gas station.

Where to take it from here...

Sometimes we feel resentful and frustrated about a disappointment, a failure, a loss, or a serious setback of some kind. We don't like it when life doesn't go as smoothly as we'd like. At those moments consider that God may be trying to get our attention, to slow us down so that we can hear his voice. Perhaps due to our frantic pace, we don't notice sin creeping into the back seat of our lives, putting us at great risk. Thank God that he's always on the lookout for us, and that at times he uses setbacks to rescue us from danger.

BIG ROCKS

In the middle of a seminar on time management, recalls Stephen Covey in his book *First Things First*, the lecturer said, "Okay, it's time for a quiz." Reaching under the table, he pulled out a widemouthed gallon jar and set it on the table next to a platter covered with fist-sized rocks. "How many of these rocks do you think we can get in the jar?" he asked the audience.

After the students made their guesses, the seminar leader said, "Okay, let's find out." He put one rock in the jar, then another, then another—until no more rocks would fit. Then he asked, "Is the jar full?"

Everybody could see that not one more of the rocks would fit, so they said, "Yes."

"Not so fast," he cautioned. From under the table he lifted out a bucket of gravel, dumped it in the jar, and shook it. The gravel slid into all the little spaces left by the big rocks. Grinning, the seminar leader asked once more, "Is the jar full?"

A little wiser by now, the students responded, "Probably not."

"Good," the teacher said. Then he reached under the table to bring up a bucket of sand. He started dumping the sand in the jar. While the students watched, the sand filled in the little spaces left by the rocks and gravel. Once more he looked at the class and said, "Now, is the jar full?"

"No," everyone shouted back.

"Good!" said the seminar leader, who then grabbed a pitcher of water and began to pour it into the jar. He got something like a quart of water into that jar before he said, "Ladies and gentlemen, the jar is now full. Can anybody tell me the lesson you can learn from this? What's my point?"

(continued)

An eager participant spoke up: "Well, there are gaps in your schedule. And if you really work at it, you can always fit more into your life."

"No," the leader said. "That's not the point. The point is this: if I hadn't put those big rocks in first, I would never have gotten them in."

Where to take it from here...

The big rocks represent our top priorities in life—the most important things we do. Jesus taught that our number one priority is to love God with all our heart, mind, and strength. Taking time each day to talk with God and listen to him is like the big rocks—if we don't get that time in right up front, all the little, less-important things will crowd out God's space in our lives. To enjoy a happy and fulfilling life, you must put the big rocks in the jar first. When you do that, you'll be surprised at how much time is left for all the little things.

Me Too!

A man was about to commit suicide by jumping from a high bridge, when a second man ran up to him shouting, "Stop! Stop! Don't do it!"

"But I have nothing to live for," said the first man.

"Maybe I can help you," said the second man. "Are you religious?"

"Yes, I am," said the first man.

"Me too!" said the second man. "Are you Christian, Jewish, or Moslem?"

"I'm Christian," said the first man.

"Me too!" said the second man. "Are you Protestant or Catholic?"

"I'm a Protestant," said the first man.

"Me too!" said the second man. "Are you Calvinist or Wesleyan?"

"Calvinist," said the first man.

"Me too!" said the second man. "Are you liberal or conservative?"

"Conservative," said the first man.

"Me too!" said the second man. "Evangelical or Fundamentalist?"

"Evangelical," said the first man.

"Me too!" said the second man. "Charismatic, Reformed, or Baptist?"

"Baptist," said the first man.

"Me too!" said the second man. "General Baptist, Conference Baptist, or Northern Baptist?"

"Conference Baptist," said the first man.

"Me too!" said the second man excitedly. "Conference Baptist of the 1932 Conference, or Conference Baptist of the 1946 Conference?"

"Conference Baptist of the 1932 Conference!" said the first man.

"1932? Then die, infidel heretic scum!" And the second man pushed the first man off the bridge.

Where to take it from here...

To categorize and stereotype each other is to hurt each other. When we spend our energy looking for what makes us different, instead of recognizing that God loves us all, we ignore God's command to love each other as we have been loved by God. Regardless of the labels we wear, we are all God's children, created in his image.

But I Have Not Yet Gone to College

The following essay was actually written by a student applying for admission to NYU in response to the question "Are there any personal accomplishments or significant experiences you have had that have helped define you as a person?" The author was accepted and is reportedly now attending college at NYU.

I am a dynamic figure, often seen scaling walls and crushing ice. I have been known to remodel train stations on my lunch breaks, making them more efficient in the area of heat retention. I translate ethnic slurs for Cuban refugees. I write award-winning operas. I manage time efficiently.

Occasionally, I tread water for three days in a row. I woo women with my sensuous and godlike trombone playing. I can pilot bicycles up severe inclines with unflagging speed, and I cook 30-minute brownies in 20 minutes.

I am an expert in stucco, a veteran in love, and an outlaw in Peru.

Using only a hoe and a large glass of water, I once single-handedly defended a small village in the Amazon basin from a horde of ferocious army ants. I play bluegrass cello. I was scouted by the Mets. I am the subject of numerous documentaries. When I'm bored, I build large suspension bridges in my yard. I enjoy urban hang gliding. On Wednesdays after school I repair electrical appliances free of charge.

I am an abstract artist, a concrete analyst, and a ruthless bookie. Critics worldwide swoon over my original line of corduroy evening wear. I don't perspire. I am a private citizen, yet I receive fan mail. I have been caller number nine and have won the weekend passes. Last summer I toured New Jersey with a traveling centrifugal force demonstration. I bat .400. My deft floral arrangements have earned me fame in international botany circles. Children trust me.

I can hurl tennis rackets at small moving objects with deadly accuracy. I once read *Paradise Lost, Moby Dick,* and *David Copperfield* in one day and still had time to refurbish an entire dining room that evening. I know the exact location of every food item in the supermarket. I have performed several covert operations for the CIA. I sleep once a week; when I do sleep, I sleep in a chair. While on vacation in Canada, I successfully negotiated with a group of terrorists who had seized a small bakery. The laws of physics do not apply to me.

I balance, I weave, I dodge, I frolic, and my bills are all paid. On weekends, to let off steam, I participate in full-contact origami. Years ago I discovered the meaning of life, but forgot to write it down. I have made extraordinary four-course meals using only a blender and a toaster oven.

I breed prize-winning clams. I have won bullfights in San Juan, cliff-diving competitions in Sri Lanka, and spelling bees at the Kremlin. I have played Hamlet, I have performed open-heart surgery, and I have spoken with Elvis.

But I have not yet gone to college.

Where to take it from here...

This young man went to great lengths to convince the admissions department at NYU that he was good enough for their school.

Are you among the many people who think you're going to have to convince God that you're good enough to get into heaven? Are you pushing yourself to accomplish as much as possible during your lifetime in order to prove to God you're worthy of eternal life?

God doesn't pay any attention to our résumés. When it comes to eternal life, our accomplishments don't make any difference. Only one thing matters: Do you know Jesus Christ? If you've let him become Lord of your life, you don't have to worry about making yourself look good—Jesus has already done that.

Onion Breath

For a long time Jerry had admired Kate—a really attractive girl who rarely dated anyone. He dreamed of dating her, but it took him weeks to work up the courage to ask her out. When he did, he was surprised at how graciously and warmly she accepted. He wished he'd asked sooner. He learned she was an outgoing person, fun to be with, and she seemed to enjoy his company.

The following week Kate readily accepted Jerry's invitation to a second date, which turned out even better than the first—until they stopped for something to eat. Embarrassed, he told her he couldn't afford much besides hamburgers. She assured him that she loved hamburgers.

Unfortunately for Jerry, she hated the smell and taste of onions. In fact, she was allergic to them. This was a real problem because Jerry just had to have onions on his hamburger! He loved onions! Suddenly faced with this dilemma, Jerry pondered what to do. Do I order onions? What's more important to me? The girl or the onions?

Kate clearly liked him and wanted to continue the relationship. She was everything he ever wanted in a girl. But to give up onions! *Boy, I sure do like onions,* Jerry thought to himself. *Maybe I can have both.*

It was time to order. He had to make a decision. "Two hamburgers, please. Hold the onions...on one of them."

Jerry never saw Kate again. She didn't return his phone calls or seek him out at school. Their relationship was clearly over. Sadly, he discovered too late that you just can't have your Kate and eat onions, too.

Some behaviors are no big deal to people. Like eating onions, as long as no one cares you're eating them, they taste good. But if eating onions offends the one you love, then eating onions is wrong.

The Bible teaches us that some things are pleasing to God and other things are not. For example, Colossians 3:20 says, "Children, obey your parents in everything, for this pleases the Lord." Of course, plenty of kids disregard that commandment and get away with it—but Christians want to please the Lord. That means they do their best to be obedient.

Do you really love the Lord? Then do what pleases him.

The Art Auction

The widowed elder man looked on with satisfaction as Mark, his only child, became an experienced art collector. The son's trained eye and sharp business mind caused his father to beam with pride as they dealt with art collectors around the world.

As winter approached war engulfed their nation, and Mark left to serve his country. After only a few short weeks, his father received a telegram: his beloved son had died saving the life of a fellow soldier. Distraught and lonely, the old man faced the upcoming Christmas holidays with anguish and sadness. The joy of the season, a season that he and his son always looked forward to, would visit his house no longer.

On Christmas morning a knock on the door awakened the old man. As he walked to the door, the masterpieces of art on the walls only reminded him that his son was not coming home. At the door was a soldier with a large package.

"I was a friend of Mark," the soldier said. "I was the one he rescued. If I may I come in for a few moments, I have something to show you."

The two were soon deep in conversation. From the soldier the old man learned that Mark had rescued dozens of wounded soldiers before a bullet stilled his caring heart. The unfolding image of his son's gallantry awakened a fatherly pride that eased his grief. The soldier then recounted how often Mark had spoken of his father's love of fine art. Placing the package on the old man's lap, the soldier told him, "I'm an artist. I want you to have this."

The old man unwrapped the package, pulling the paper away to reveal a portrait of his son. The canvas featured the young man's face in striking detail, though the world would never consider the painting the work of a genius. Overcome with emotion, the man thanked the soldier.

Once the soldier had departed, the old man set about hanging the portrait above the fireplace, pushing aside paintings by masters that had cost thousands of dollars. Then seating himself in his chair, he spent Christmas gazing at the gift he had been given. In the weeks that followed, the man grew peaceful realizing that Mark lived on because of those he had touched. The soldier's gift soon became his most prized painting, its worth to him far eclipsing the value of the pieces in his collection for which museums around the world clamored. He told his neighbors it was the greatest gift he had ever received.

The following spring, the old man became ill and passed away. The art world stirred in anticipation of the public auction of the old man's estate. He had stipulated that his collection be sold on Christmas day—the day he had received his greatest gift. On the appointed day art collectors from around the world gathered to bid on the spectacular paintings. Many who coveted the reputation of owning the greatest art collection waited eagerly for the auctioneer to open the bidding.

The auction began with a painting not on any museum's must-have list—the soldier's painting of the old man's son. "May I have an opening bid," the auctioneer requested. The room was silent. "Who will open the bidding with $100?" he prompted. Minutes passed and still no one spoke.

"Who cares about that painting?" shouted a bidder from the back of the room. "It's just a picture of his son," commented another. More voices echoed agreement. "Let's forget it and go on to the good stuff."

"No, we have to sell this one first," replied the auctioneer. "Now, who will take the son?"

Finally, a friend of the old man spoke. "I'd like to have the painting. I knew the boy. Will you take ten dollars for it? That's all I have."

"I have ten dollars," called the auctioneer. "Will anyone go higher?" More silence. "Going once." The auctioneer raised the gavel. "Going twice," he said looking around for any takers. "Gone," he said at last, letting the gavel fall.

Cheers filled the room. "Now we can get on with bidding on these treasures!" remarked the man from the back of the room.

Over the microphone the auctioneer said. "Thank you for coming. The auction is now over." Stunned disbelief quieted the room.

"What do you mean it's over?" growled an irate bidder.

"We didn't come here for a picture of some old guy's son!" said another.

"What about all of these other paintings?" shouted the irate bidder coming to his feet. "There are millions of dollars of art here! I demand that you explain what's going on!"

(continued)

"It's very simple," replied the auctioneer. "According to the will of the father, whoever takes the son...gets it all."

And that is the will of the Father today. Whoever takes the Son...gets it all. When you take Christ as Savior, you will have the riches of life to its fullest (John 10:10, Matthew 6:33). Jesus is God's greatest treasure, his pearl of great price (Matthew 13:45–46).

JENNY

Jenny was 13 and wild. Everyone agreed that she got wilder each passing month. Taller and more physically mature than many of her friends, she found it easy to attract older guys by merely tossing back her long, strawberry-blonde hair and giving a faint smile. She was experienced in all the vices the world could dangle before her. Considering her home life, it would have been amazing if she had turned out any other way. Her father, long out of the picture, had left her with her drug-using mother who, in a warped attempt at bonding, actually provided drugs to Jenny so they could get high together.

Somehow, in spite of the blur of sex, drugs, and alcohol abuse, Jenny agreed to go with a friend to a junior high game night put on by a local church. Even though she didn't return in the following weeks, something in the youth pastor's short message found its way into her mind. He told a story about a prostitute, so sorry about the way she was living that she cried at the feet of Jesus and wiped his feet dry with her hair.

Several years passed. Jenny grew more out of control, "raging" night after night.

In the middle of the night, a very stoned Jenny and her small clutch of girlfriends roamed the back roads of their little town after a party, when God began to break through to Jenny. Suddenly the guilt, self-loathing, and despair that had been pressed down and layered with numbing narcotics for so long exploded in her mind. She was sick of her life, ashamed of her behavior, and she desperately wanted God.

"Perhaps a church could help," she reasoned, not considering that at two in the morning no one would likely be there who could help her. Breaking from her group of friends, Jenny made her way to the nearest church, a magnificent Catholic church set in finely manicured grounds.

Then she saw him. It was Jesus. He was standing on top of a concrete pad in a small garden next to the parking lot. His arms were outstretched. Jenny went to him.

(continued)

Jenny dropped on her knees in front of this life-sized statue of Jesus and began to weep. Then the story she had heard years ago came to her. With tears of repentance she washed the feet of the statue, and with her long hair she dried off the immovable feet.

For a few moments the act of a broken heart made the feet of the statue as real as if they had been the very feet of the Savior himself.

Where to take it from here...

The arms of Jesus are also outstretched for you. If you come to him, he will forgive you for your sins, release you from your guilt, and give you eternal life. He is not a statue in a garden but a living, risen Savior who wants to be your constant friend and companion.

Don't wait until you hit rock bottom like Jenny did. Come to Jesus today.

Come Home

Max Lucado tells this story in his book *No Wonder They Call Him Savior*:

The small house was simple but adequate. It consisted of one large room on a dusty street. Its red-tiled roof was one of many in this poor neighborhood on the outskirts of the Brazilian village. It was a comfortable home. Maria and her daughter, Christina, had done what they could to add color to the gray walls and warmth to the hard dirt floor: an old calendar, a faded photograph of a relative, a wooden crucifix. The furnishings were modest: a pallet on either side of the room, a washbasin, and a wood-burning stove.

Maria's husband had died when Christina was an infant. The young mother, stubbornly refusing opportunities to remarry, got a job and set out to raise her young daughter. And now, fifteen years later, the worst years were over. Though Maria's salary as a maid afforded few luxuries, it was reliable and it did provide food and clothes. And now, Christina was old enough to get a job to help out.

Some said Christina got her independence from her mother. She recoiled at the traditional idea of marrying young and raising a family. Not that she couldn't have had her pick of husbands. Her olive skin and brown eyes kept a steady stream of prospects at her door. She had an infectious way of throwing her head back and filling the room with laughter. She also had that rare magic some women have that makes every man feel like a king just by being near them. But it was her spirited curiosity that made her keep all the men at arm's length.

She spoke often of going to the city. She dreamed of trading her dusty neighborhood for exciting avenues and city life. Just the thought of this horrified her mother. Maria was always quick to remind Christina of the harshness of the streets. "People don't know you there. Jobs are scarce and the life is cruel. And besides, if you went there, what would you do for a living?"

Maria knew exactly what Christina would do, or would *have* to do for a living. That's why her heart broke when she awoke one morning to find her daughter's bed empty. Maria knew immediately where her daughter had gone. She also knew immediately what she must do to find her. She quickly threw some clothes in a bag, gathered up all her money and ran out of the house.

On her way to the bus stop she entered a drugstore to get one last thing. Pictures. She sat in the photograph booth, closed the curtain, and spent all she could on pictures of herself. With her purse full of small black and white photos, she boarded the next bus to Rio de Janeiro.

Maria knew Christina had no way of earning money. She also knew that her daughter was too stubborn to give up. When pride meets hunger, a human will do things that were before unthinkable. Knowing this, Maria began her search. Bars, hotels, nightclubs, any place with a reputation for streetwalkers or prostitutes. She went to them all. And at each place she left her picture—taped to a hotel bulletin board, fastened to a corner phone booth. And on the back of each photo, she wrote a note.

It wasn't too long before both the money and the pictures ran out, and Maria had to go home. The weary mother wept as the bus began its long journey back to her small village.

It was a few weeks later that young Christina descended the hotel stairs. Her face was tired. Her brown eyes no longer danced with youth but spoke of pain and fear. Her laughter was broken. Her dream had become a nightmare. A thousand times over she had longed to trade these countless beds for her secure pallet. Yet the little village was, in too many ways, too far away.

As she reached the bottom of the stairs, her eyes noticed a familiar face. She looked again, and there on the lobby mirror was a small picture of her mother. Christina's eyes burned and her throat tightened as she walked across the room and removed the small photo. Written on the back was this compelling invitation: "Whatever you have done, whatever you have become, it doesn't matter. Please come home."

She did.

Where to take it from here...

Jesus is God's picture taped to a Roman cross, inviting us to come home. "The Son is the radiance of God's glory and the exact representation of his being..." (Hebrews 1:3). When you look at Jesus, you can't help but see the Father who loves you. No matter what you've done, no matter what you've become, God invites you to come home. "Come to me, all you who are weary and burdened, and I will give you rest" (Matthew 11:28).

Praise in the Dugout

Orel Herschiser pitched an unbelievable 1988 season for the Los Angeles Dodgers. Following a complete game shutout in August, he pitched multiple shutout innings and hurled five more complete games through the end of the regular season. He did not allow his opponents to score an earned run in 59 consecutive innings.

When the Dodgers faced the New York Mets in the National League play-offs, Orel continued to dominate hitters, leading the Dodgers to victory by pitching more than 24 innings, crowned by a complete game shutout in the final game! In the World Series his complete game victory over the Oakland A's in game five clinched the series for the Dodgers. No wonder Orel was awarded the Cy Young award and two MVP awards, one for the National League play-offs and the other for the World Series.

During the play-offs the TV cameras zoomed in on this legend in the making. They caught Orel in the dugout between innings singing softly to himself. Unable to make out the tune, the announcers merely commented that Orel's record certainly gave him something to sing about.

Johnny Carson replayed that tape on the "Tonight Show" a few days later when Orel appeared. Johnny asked him what song he had been singing during the game and if Orel would sing it again right then and there. The audience roared its approval over Orel's embarrassed reluctance.

(continued)

So on national TV, Orel softly sang the tune TV crews had barely caught on tape:

"Praise God from whom all blessings flow.
Praise Him all creatures here below;
Praise Him above ye heavenly host,
Praise Father, Son and Holy Ghost. Amen."

Where to take it from here...

Orel Herschiser was simply doing what Christians do—praising God for everything that he'd achieved. Paul urges the Colossians, "Whatever you do...do it all in the name of the Lord Jesus, giving thanks to God the Father through him" (3:17). Not only at church, but in the in-between moments, thank God for your gifts and talents—he gave them to you.

Psychiatric Hot Line

A man experiencing a crisis in his life called the toll-free Psychiatric Hot Line listed in the phone directory. This is what he heard:

"Welcome to the Psychiatric Hot Line.
- If you are obsessive-compulsive, repeatedly press 1.
- If you are codependent, ask someone to press 2.
- If you have multiple personalities, press 3, 4, and 5.
- If you are suffering from paranoia, we know who you are and what you want. Stay on the line until we trace the call.
- If you are schizophrenic, listen carefully and a little voice will tell you which number to press.
- If you are bipolar, it doesn't matter which number you press. No one will answer.
- If you are depressed, push any button you wish. It won't make any difference anyhow.

Thank you for your call."

Where to take it from here...

Next time you need help, keep in mind that God always hears and answers your prayers. When you call on God, you aren't going to get a voice-mail system, nor will you be put on hold. God wants you to come to him every day to tell him what's on your mind.

And if you're in the middle of a crisis, remember that you're not the only one who can pray you through it—people in your church will pray with you and for you. That's why the church is called the Body of Christ. The church is the visible presence of Jesus in the world, providing advice and support based on Jesus' teaching. In the same way that Jesus cares about you, members of your church care. Professional counseling is appropriate, of course, when you face serious problems; but Christians have been commanded to "carry each other's burdens" (Galatians 6:2).

DUH...

How many of these questions can you answer correctly?

1. Do they have a fourth of July in England?
2. How many birthdays does the average man have?
3. Some months have 31 days. How many have 28?
4. A woman gives a beggar 50 cents; the woman is the beggar's sister, but the beggar is not the woman's brother. How come?
5. Why can't a man living in the U.S.A. be buried in Canada?
6. How may outs are there in an inning?
7. Is it legal for a man in California to marry his widow's sister? Why?
8. Two men play five games of checkers. Each man wins the same number of games. There are no ties. Explain this.
9. Divide 30 by one-half and add 10. What is the answer?
10. A man builds a house which is rectangular in shape. All four sides have a southern exposure. A big bear walks by. What color is the bear?
11. If there are three apples and you take away two, how many do you have?
12. I have two U.S. coins totaling 55 cents. One isn't a nickel. What are the coins?
13. If you had only one match and you walked into a room where there was a candle, a kerosene lamp, and a wood burning stove, which would you light first?
14. How far can a dog run into the woods?
15. A doctor gives you three pills, telling you to take one every half hour. How long will the pills last?
16. A farmer has 17 sheep, and all but 9 die. How many are left?
17. How many animals of each sex did Moses take on the ark?
18. A clerk in the butcher shop is 5 feet, 10 inches tall. What does he weigh?
19. How many two-cent stamps are there in a dozen?

Still More Hot Illustrations for Youth Talks

20. What was the President's name in 1950?
21. How much dirt is in a hole three feet wide by five feet long by four feet deep?
22. You are driving a train eastbound on a railroad track at 60 miles per hour. You travel for 30 minutes and pick up ten passengers. Thirty minutes later all but three of the passengers get off the train. What is the engineer's name?

Answers

1. Yes. They also have a third of July, a second of July, etc.
2. One a year.
3. All months have (at least) 28 days.
4. The beggar is the woman's sister.
5. Because he is living.
6. Six—three per side.
7. No—the man would be dead.
8. They are not playing each other.
9. 70—to divide by one-half, multiply by 2: 30 times 2 equals 60 plus 10 equals 70.
10. White. It's a polar bear because the house was built on the North Pole.
11. Two—you just took two apples.
12. A 50-cent piece and a nickel. One is not a nickel, but the other one is.
13. Light the match first.
14. Half way. Then he would be running out.
15. One hour. You take the first pill, then a half hour later, the second one, then an hour after taking the first one, you take the third pill.
16. Nine—all but nine die.
17. None—Moses was not on the ark.
18. He weighs meat.
19. 12.
20. Bill Clinton. (Or whoever the current president is—assuming he was alive in 1950.)
21. None—it's a hole.
22. Whatever your name is. You are driving the train.

(continued)

Where to take it from here...

Taking this quiz illustrates how critical it is to listen. Those who listened with discernment when the questions were read answered every one of them correctly. Those who didn't listen closely found themselves stumped on quite a few, merely guessing at the answers and making errors.

In life we also find ourselves stumped or making wrong choices in life because we haven't listened with attention. God speaks to us through his Word and through people who care about us. To be successful in life, we need to become discerning listeners.

Read All about It!

Actual headlines from real newspapers:

- Grandmother of Eight Makes Hole in One
- Police Begin Campaign to Run Down Jaywalkers
- House Passes Gas Tax onto Senate
- Stiff Opposition Expected to Funeral Plan
- Two Convicts Evade Noose, Jury Hung
- Milk Drinkers Are Turning to Powder
- Safety Experts Say Children on School Bus Should Be Belted
- Iraqi Head Seeks Arms
- Queen Mary Having Bottom Scraped
- Panda Mating Fails, Veterinarian Takes Over
- Child's Stool Great for Use in Garden
- Eye Drops Off Shelf
- Squad Helps Dog Bite Victim
- Dealers Will Hear Car Talk at Noon
- Two Sisters Reunite after Eighteen Years at Checkout Counter
- Man Is Fatally Slain
- Something Went Wrong in Jet Crash, Experts Say
- Juvenile Court to Try Shooting Defendant
- Stolen Painting Found by Tree
- Red Tape Holds Up New Bridge
- Astronaut Takes Blame for Gas in Spacecraft
- Kids Make Nutritious Snacks
- Local High School Dropouts Cut in Half
- Sex Education Delayed, Teachers Request Training

(continued)

We've all had times when what we write or say just comes out wrong. When we share Christ with people, for instance, what do they hear in our stumbling attempts at proclaiming the gospel? What we mean to say is sometimes not what actually comes out. Listen to yourself; make sure you're not communicating a wrong impression of what it means to be a Christian.

Donuts at the Back

I was holding a notice from my 13-year-old son's school announcing a meeting to preview the new course in sexuality. Parents could examine the curriculum and take part in an actual lesson presented exactly as it would be given to the students.

Arriving at the school, I was surprised to discover only about a dozen parents gathered, waiting for the presentation. I picked up a teacher guide and thumbed through page after page of instructions in the prevention of pregnancy or disease. Abstinence was mentioned only in passing.

When the teacher arrived with the school nurse, she asked if there were any questions. I asked why abstinence did not play a noticeable part in the material. What happened next shocked me. Speaking over a great deal of laughter, someone suggested that if I thought abstinence had any merit, I should go back to burying my head in the sand. The teacher and the nurse said nothing as I drowned in a sea of embarrassment. My mind had gone blank, and I could think of nothing to say. The teacher explained to me that the job of the school was to teach facts; the home was responsible for moral training. I sat in silence for the next 20 minutes as she explained the course to parents who seemed to give their unqualified support to the materials.

"Donuts at the back," announced the teacher during the break. "I'd like you to put on the name tags we've prepared—they're right by the donuts— and mingle with the other parents." Everyone moved to the back of the room. As I watched them affixing their name tags and shaking hands, I sat deep in thought. I was ashamed that I had not been able to convince them to include a serious discussion of abstinence in the materials.

I uttered a silent prayer for guidance. My thoughts were interrupted by the teacher's hand on my shoulder. "Won't you join the others, Mr. Daniels?"

(continued)

The nurse smiled sweetly at me. "The donuts are good."

"Thank you, no," I replied.

"Well then, how about a name tag? I'm sure the others would like to meet you."

"Somehow I doubt that," I replied.

"Won't you please join them?" she coaxed. Then I heard a still, small voice whisper, "Don't go." The instruction was unmistakable. "Don't go!"

"I'll just wait here," I said.

The teacher called the class back to order and, looking around the long table, thanked everyone for putting on name tags. She ignored me. "Now we're going to give you the same lesson we'll be giving your children," she began. "Everyone, please peel off your name tags." I watched in silence as the tags came off. "Now then, on the back of one of the tags, I drew a tiny flower. Who has it, please?"

The gentleman across from me held it up. "Here it is!"

"All right," she said. "The flower represents disease. Do you recall with whom you shook hands?" He pointed to a couple of people. "Very good," she replied. "The handshake in this case represents intimacy. So the two people you had contact with now have the disease." That produced another round of laughter and witty comments.

"And with whom did the two of you shake hands?" the teacher continued. She had made her point. "This demonstrates for students how quickly disease is spread. Since we all shook hands, we all have the disease."

At that moment I heard again the still, small voice. "Speak now," it said, "but be humble." Noting wryly the latter admonition, I rose from my chair and apologized for any upset I might have caused earlier. I then congratulated the teacher on an excellent lesson that would impress the youth and concluded by saying I had only one small point I wished to make.

"Not all of us were infected," I said. "One of us...abstained."

— *Author unknown*

Where to take it from here...

When you are tempted to do what you know is wrong, listen for that still, small voice. It will likely be the voice of the Holy Spirit (John 14:26) prompting you to obey God. And when you obey, you will have nothing to regret.

Sammy's Big Catch

Sammy was a good-looking young boy who lived in the deep south. His summer days were filled with times of walking through the woods, playing with friends, and fishing in the pond down the dirt road. Fishing was by far his favorite thing to do. Just about every day during his summer vacation, he would dig up some worms and head off, pole in hand, for a day of fishing.

This steamy hot day was like most others during Sammy's summer break. Waking early, he could hear the pond calling him to come fish. Sammy quietly walked out the front door, grabbed his pitchfork and worm pail from the porch, and walked into the woods to search for bait. He turned over old stumps and dug under leaves hoping to find worms. Under one old stump he hit the jackpot. The ground was writhing. In two minutes he had all the bait he needed, and in 15 minutes he was at the pond.

Reaching into his bait bucket, Sammy pulled out a big worm. He double hooked it and tossed it into the water. He noticed a stinging in his hand, but filled with the excitement of the moment, he paid no attention to it. Within 30 seconds, Sammy had a strike and pulled in a nice catfish. Wow, he thought, a fish in the first minute. This is unbelievable!

He put the catch on his stringer, hurried to rebait his hook, and tried his luck again. Once again he felt a stinging sensation in his hand as he threw his hook into the pond. He didn't have time to worry about it. Within just a few seconds, he had another huge fish. He fumbled the next time he baited his hook—his hand felt numb and stiff. But Sammy was too excited about catching another fish to give it much thought.

At the end of only an hour of fishing, Sammy had caught eight large fish. This was definitely his best fishing day ever. He was so proud of his accomplishment that, even though there was plenty of day left to fish, he threw the heavy stringer of fish over his shoulder and dashed down the dirt road toward home to show off his catch to his mom and dad.

The local sheriff happened to drive up alongside Sammy and started

to congratulate him on his catch of fish. With a smile and a victory whoop, Sammy held up the stringer. The sheriff gasped, parked his car and strode over to Sammy. His eyes hadn't deceived him—Sammy's arms really were red and swollen to about twice their normal size.

"Exactly where have you been and what bait did you use to catch all those fish?" the sheriff asked Sammy, already guessing the answer.

"I found some special bait under an old stump," Sammy boasted. "These worms really wiggle good," he commented, handing up the bait bucket for inspection. After a close look at the worms, the sheriff went into fast-forward. Securing the bucket in his truck, he then scooped Sammy and his stringer of fish into the backseat of his patrol car. Spinning a U-turn on the gravel road, he sped off to the hospital, but Sammy was already dead.

What the sheriff had discovered was that Sammy had been fishing with baby rattlesnakes.

Where to take it from here...

Sammy's deadly bait brought him a good morning's fishing but cost him his life. Had Sammy stopped fishing after that first sting, he could have been saved. One bite from a baby rattler won't kill a person who gets treatment in time. But Sammy was having fun and didn't bother himself with the small voice of pain in his hand. Then, as his hand grew numb, even that small voice was silenced.

Playing around with sin is like using baby rattlesnakes for bait. Sinning seems harmless to young people who don't recognize sin and are unaware of its deadly consequences. The more sin you get into, however, the more numb you become to its sting. In the excitement of the moment, you ignore the still small voice of God warning you of danger and encouraging you to choose life instead of death.

The River

Walking through the forest, a seasoned hiker came upon a broad, slowly moving river. He stopped to gaze over the waters, appreciating the beauty, when suddenly he heard a faint cry coming from upstream. Looking in the direction of the noise, he saw an obviously drowning man floundering in the river and drifting slowly toward him.

The hiker was stunned momentarily, but he sprang into action when he saw the man disappear beneath the waters. Throwing off all of his cumbersome gear, he dove into the river and swam like a madman toward the spot where the man went under.

Upon reaching the spot he plunged below the surface and frantically hauled up the helpless man. Then he laboriously towed the victim to shore. Heaving the lifeless body up on the riverbank, the hiker attempted to revive the man, who eventually spit up water and began to breathe.

Relieved, the hiker paused to catch his breath. But no sooner had he done so than he heard another voice out on the water. Another drowning person! Once again he swam out and pulled the person to shore, a little more slowly this time. As the hiker-turned-lifeguard revived the second victim, he heard yet another cry for help.

All day long the hiker worked, rescuing one person after another as they came drifting down the river. There seemed to be no end of drowning victims, and the hiker didn't think he could keep it up.

Just when he was about to collapse from exhaustion, he spotted another man walking rapidly beside the river, headed upstream. "Hey mister!" he cried out. "Please help me! These poor people are drowning!"

Amazingly, the man kept walking upstream. The astonished hiker called out again. Without even acknowledging the cry, the man kept going. Indignant and angry, the hiker leapt to his feet, ran toward the uncompassionate man, stood directly in his path, and in a loud voice demanded, "Sir! How can you possibly walk past all these drowning people? Have you no conscience? Must I force you to help me save these people?"

(continued)

The stranger stopped, looked at him for the first time and said with a calm, focused voice, "Sir, please get out of my way. I am headed upstream to stop the guy who is pushing all these people in."

Where to take it from here...

Each of us has a role to play in rescuing those who are drowning in sin. Some of us pull people from the water and resuscitate them with counseling, food and shelter, a rehabilitation program, a support group, or financial aid. Affirm those doing these important ministries.

Others of us find our place of ministry upstream, opposing the one pushing people into the river. We do this by introducing those people to Jesus Christ. Knowing Christ sets a person free from sin and releases them from Satan's power over them.

By itself, pulling people from the water isn't enough. We need to help people deal with the problem of sin at its source.

The Saucer

San Francisco is home to hundreds of little stores that sell both worthless junk and valuable antiques. Savvy shoppers can find some real treasures among all the debris.

One day an antique connoisseur walked into one of these stores. Browsing the items for sale, he came across an unremarkable cat drinking milk from a saucer on the floor. The man immediately recognized this saucer as genuine Ming Dynasty, worth hundreds of thousands of dollars. And here it was on the floor, with a cat drinking milk out of it! The shop owner obviously did not know its worth.

Immediately, the man started scheming how to get it for cheap, without the shopkeeper knowing what he was selling. He turned to the shopkeeper and said, "You know, that's a very striking cat you have there. I'd really like to buy your cat."

"Well," answered the shopkeeper, "the cat is not really for sale."

"I insist," the man replied. "Would you take $100 for the cat?"

"That's very generous," said the shopkeeper with a shake of his head. "I don't think this cat is worth $100, but if you want the cat that badly, you can have it."

The man paid for the cat and then, as if he'd just thought of it, said, "Oh, one more thing. I'm going to need something to use as a feeding dish for the cat, so I'll give you another $5 for that little saucer there on the floor."

"Oh, I could never do that," said the shopkeeper. "You see, that's no ordinary saucer. That's a piece of rare china from the Ming Dynasty and its worth is incalculable. But amazingly enough, ever since I started feeding my cats out of it, I've sold 12 cats."

(continued)

That shopkeeper degraded something of great value to upgrade the worth of his cats. God also used something of great value to redeem us and to give us life—Christ, who was degraded on the cross so that we could be upgraded to eternal life. As a result, we have become priceless treasures.

On the other hand, customers who didn't know any better walked by the cat's milk dish without realizing that they were walking past a treasure. Next time you walk past what look like ordinary persons, don't be fooled. They're treasures—people God loves so much that he sacrificed his Son on their behalf.

How to Train an Elephant

Have you ever wondered how to train an elephant? The first step is making it believe it can't run away.

Get your elephant—preferably a baby one—and tie it to a strong steel stake in the ground, like you would tie a horse to a hitching post. The baby elephant will try to break free, but it won't have the strength to do so. Eventually, the little elephant will give up and stop trying to escape from the rope and the stake that limit its range.

Once the young elephant has learned that it cannot pull the stake from the ground, you can replace the strong stake with a smaller wooden one, even though it wouldn't have enough strength to hold the elephant. An elephant trained in its babyhood to believe that the stake is strong and won't budge won't attempt to break loose and run away—even after it has grown strong enough to easily yank almost any stake out of the ground.

Where to take it from here...

We are also best trained in our youth by a strong stake in the ground that teaches us where the limits are, by a certainty about the difference between right and wrong. That stake is the Word of God. The only way you can become an obedient follower of Jesus is to submit yourself to the authority of the Word of God. And you need to start now! The Bible teaches you to "remember your Creator in the days of your youth" (Ecclesiastes 12:1). If you discipline yourself now, you'll be able to control yourself when truly difficult times of temptation come your way.

God's Nickel

Back in the days when you could still buy an ice cream cone for a nickel, there was a little boy who lived in a small town with his grandmother. Every Sunday the grandmother took the boy to church and after they would go downtown for a special treat—an ice cream cone. One Sunday grandmother was not feeling well, and she told the boy that he would have to go to church by himself. Before he left she gave him two nickels—one for the offering plate and one for an ice cream after church.

Now it happened that the boy needed to cross an old wooden bridge in order to get to church. As he was crossing the old bridge, he began jumping up and down, as boys will do, making the bridge shake and sway. His sharp ears picked up a small *thunk,* and he looked down just in time to see one of the nickels his grandmother had given him roll into a small crack on the bridge. The little boy fell down on all fours and put his eye to the crack. He watched helplessly as the nickel fell into the river below.

Standing up and dusting off his knees, he said to no one in particular, "Oh well. There goes God's nickel."

Where to take it from here...

Often when we're low on money, it's God who doesn't get his share. If we run out of time, then God waits in vain for us to be with him. If we run out of energy, then God's work suffers.

Jesus turned those kinds of priorities upside down when he said, "Seek first his kingdom and his righteousness, and all these things will be given to you" (Matthew 6:33). If you will give God the first and best of all that you have, then God will bless you with all that you need and more!

King of the Universe

A doctor at a mental institution was making his rounds one evening when he heard shouting from one of the cells.

"I am the King of the Universe! I am the Ruler of the World! From now on everyone will do what I say because I am the Supreme Commander of the Galaxies!"

The doctor investigated, opening a door to find a man in his skivvies, standing on a chair, beating his chest and yelling, "I am the King of the Universe!"

"Harry!" interrupted the doctor over the man's shouting. "Harry, get down off that chair! And quiet down! You're disrupting people who are trying to sleep!"

"I am the King of the Universe!"

"Harry, you are not the King of the Universe!"

"Yes I am!" he cried all the louder.

"And just what makes you think you are King of the Universe?" asked the doctor.

"*God told me* I was King of the Universe!" shouted Harry.

Just then a voice erupted from another cell down the hallway: "I did not!"

Where to take it from here...

You know the type. They may not exactly claim to be God, but they're convinced that God has given them the final word on what's true and not true, what's right and what's wrong. Are they candidates for mental institutions, or simply deluded? Is ego or ambition a factor? Or is it an understandable need for certainty and firm answers in a world filled with theories and opinions that are constantly changing?

New York Power

Still fresh in the memory of many is the huge power failure that involved much of the northeast United States in November 1965. At 5:18 p.m. New York City went black. So did some 80,000 square miles of New York state, most of seven other states, and most of Canada's province of Ontario. Whether the cause was a generator feeding power at the wrong frequency or a switch thrown in error by some utility company employee was hard to determine.

Millions of people living in New York and the surrounding area had no light and no power, and many of them were stuck for the night in subway train stations, office buildings, and in tunnels under the East River. The blackout meant some 200 planes in the air above New York's Kennedy International Airport had to be rerouted to air fields in other states where runway lights were still burning. Overall loss in business due to the blackout, which lasted in some areas up to 13 hours, was estimated at $100,000,000. A tire company, for example, lost $50,000 worth of tires when power failed during a critical curing process. A car manufacturer had to throw away 50 engine blocks because high-speed drills froze while boring piston holes. Bakeries in New York alone reported a loss of 300,000 loaves of bread, which were spoiled when the power went off.

All in all, modern civilization as Americans and Canadians knew it came to a halt that November night because the power supply on which they depended had been cut off.

Where to take it from here...

Christians have a power supply on which we are completely dependent—the Holy Spirit (John 16:8-15). The Holy Spirit not only convicts you of sin, but also leads you into all truth and gives you the confidence and power that you need to live a successful Christian life.

When you "cut off the current," however, by quenching the Holy Spirit (1 Thessalonians 5:19), your power stops. Just as New Yorkers groped around in darkened subways and tunnels under the East River during that paralyzing blackout, anyone who dims the power of the Holy Spirit in his or her life has no sure sense of spiritual direction.

Unlike the victims of the 1965 power failure, though, you don't have to wait for hours for someone to turn the power back on. You can turn on the spiritual lights any time you want by throwing the switch marked "obedience."

A Special Special Olympics

The president of the Special Olympics was giving a talk to a large audience. During the question and answer time that followed, someone asked him to describe the best moment for him as president of that year's Special Olympics. Without any hesitation he told about the 100-meter run.

Six developmentally handicapped kids lined up in a stadium filled with 50,000 people. These kids had prepared all year for this event. They wanted to win. Although they could not run well, they would give it their very best effort.

The gun went off and all six began to run. At about the 50-meter mark, one of the six runners fell down, face first on the track. The other five runners took a couple more steps and then stopped. They looked back and saw the fallen runner. Then, to the surprise of the crowd, they all went back, helped the fallen runner to his feet, joined hands, and continued the race—all of them crossing the finish line at the same moment.

Each one received a gold medal.

Where to take it from here...

Our role as members of Jesus' church is helping those who fall to get back up. The church is not the place for competition; we must serve together in unity. What Jesus wanted most of all for the church was that we would be one (John 17:23).

The Ballad of the Oyster

There once was an oyster
Whose story I tell,
Who found that some sand
Had got into its shell.

It was only a grain,
But it gave him great pain;
For oysters have feelings
Although they're so plain.

Now, did he berate
The harsh workings of fate
That had brought him
To such a deplorable state?

Did he curse at the government,
Cry for election,
And claim that the sea should
Have given him protection?

No! He said to himself
As he lay on a shell,
"Since I cannot remove it,
I'll try to improve it."

Now the years have rolled by,
As the years always do,

And he came to his ultimate
Destiny—stew.

And the small grain of sand
That had bothered him so
Was a beautiful pearl
All richly aglow.

Now the tale has a moral;
For isn't it grand
What an oyster can do
With a small grain of sand?

What couldn't we do
If we'd only begin
With some of the things
That get under our skin.

Where to take it from here...

Remember that every pearl got its start irritating an oyster. "In all things God works for the good of those who love him, who have been called according to his purpose" (Romans 8:28).

SLEEPING WITH A MONKEY

A man came home to discover that his wife had bought a pet monkey.

"You bought a monkey?" the incredulous man asked. "Where will the monkey sleep?"

"In our bed—with us," said the wife.

"But what about the odor?" asked the man.

"Well, *I* got used to you," said the wife, "I guess the monkey can too."

Where to take it from here...

Before you criticize others, be sure that the problem is not in fact yours. Jesus taught, "Why do you look at the speck of sawdust in your brother's eye and pay no attention to the plank in your own eye?" (Matthew 7:3).

The Graduation Gift

About to graduate from high school, a young man from a wealthy family was anticipating his gift. It was the custom in that affluent neighborhood for the parents to give the graduate a new car.

Jason and his father had spent months looking at cars, and the week before graduation they found the perfect car. Jason was certain that this car would be his on graduation night. Imagine his disappointment when, immediately following the graduation ceremony, Jason's father handed him a small, elegantly wrapped package. It must be the keys to my new car, Jason thought.

Upon opening the gift, though, all he found was a Bible with his name imprinted on the front. A Bible? He took it out, looking to find car keys in the box. Empty! Jason was so angry that he threw the Bible down and stormed out of the house. His father tried to stop him, but Jason kept on running. He and his father never saw each other again.

News of his father's death finally brought Jason home again. As he went through the possessions he was about to inherit from his father, he came across the graduation Bible. Brushing away the dust, he opened it and began idly flipping through the pages. A paper tucked inside caught his eye and he pulled out of the Bible a cashier's check, dated the day of his graduation, in the exact amount of the car he and his father had chosen.

Where to take it from here...

Stay close to God and he will give you the desires of your heart. The Bible is full of treasures. "Seek first his kingdom and his righteousness and all these things will be given to you." (Matthew 6:33) Open it; read it; apply it.

A Mickey Mouse Trip

Jeremy wore inch-thick, coke-bottle glasses and a perfect bowl haircut. He knew the answers to everything and was the teacher's pet. This really ticked everybody off.

One day, after an uncharacteristic absence from school, Jeremy showed up in class with a big grin on his face, wearing a goofy-looking Mickey Mouse hat. The teacher asked Jeremy where he got the hat.

"I went to Disneyland yesterday!" he said excitedly.

"Oh really," said the teacher. "Why don't you tell us about your trip to Disneyland."

"Okay! Well, I got to Disneyland and the first thing I saw was the parking lot," Jeremy said. "That parking lot must hold about a million cars! I got on a tram that carried me around the parking lot until I got to the place where you buy the tickets. So I got off and stood in line. I bought a ticket and I also bought this cool hat!"

"And then what did you do?" asked the teacher.

"Well, I got back on the tram and rode around the parking lot some more," said Jeremy. "That was really fun! I rode that tram all day!"

"All day?" asked the teacher. "Did you go through the turnstiles and under the bridge to Main Street U.S.A., Adventureland, Fantasyland, Tomorrowland, and the rest of the park?"

Jeremy thought for a moment and said, "No. Was I supposed to?"

Where to take it from here...

Makes you wonder what they teach kids in grade school these days. Jeremy never experienced the fun of Disneyland because he never went beyond the ticket booth. He had his ticket in his hand and could have gone in any time. Instead, he settled for a ride around the parking lot, watching happy people come out of Disneyland with smiles on their faces. But he never found out what they were smiling about.

Have you "bought a ticket to heaven" by inviting Christ into your life? Have you gotten past the ticket booth? Or are you still riding around the

parking lot, feeling like you may be missing out on all that Christ has for you? We hear other Christians talk about the joy they experience as a follower of Jesus, but sometimes we are clueless.

Don't settle for merely watching other Christians experience their walk with God. Experience it for yourself.

STAGES OF A COLD

How does a typical husband respond when his wife comes down with a cold?

In the first year of marriage: "Sugar Dumpling, I'm really worried about my baby girl. You've got a bad sniffle, and there's no telling about these things with all the terrible viruses that are going around these days. I'm taking you to the hospital, Dear, where I've reserved a private room for you. I know the food's lousy, so I'll be bringing your meals in from Rozzini's. I've already made all the arrangements with the floor superintendent."

Second year of marriage: "Listen, Darling, I don't like the sound of that cough and I've called the doctor to rush right over. Now you go to bed like a good girl, and I'll take care of everything."

Third year: "Maybe you'd better lie down, Honey. Nothing like a little rest when you're feeling lousy. I'll bring you something. Do we have any canned soup?"

Fourth year: "Now look, Dear, be sensible. After you feed the kids, do the dishes, and mop the floor, you'd better get some rest."

Fifth year: "Why don't you take a couple aspirin?"

Sixth year: "If you'd just gargle or something instead of sitting around barking like a seal all night..."

Seventh year: "For Pete's sake, stop that sneezing! What are you trying to do, give me pneumonia?"

Where to take it from here...

Love has a way of growing cold unless we work hard to keep it fresh and alive. That's true in our human relationships and also in our relationship with God. Our relationship with God takes the same kind of commitment and effort required for a good marriage. The difference is that even though our love for God grows and shrinks with our whims, God's love for us never changes. He doesn't get tired of us or start taking us for granted. He loves us every day just like the first. His love knows no measure; it is overflowing and without end (Ephesians 2:4-5; Romans 5:8).

Star Light, Star Bright

Use the following illustration as an object lesson in a room where you can create complete darkness:

Prepare ahead:
- Prepare a message for your youth about how we need to spend time with Jesus, the Light of the World, so that we can become light for our dark world.
- Purchase a set of glow-in-the-dark plastic stars. You can find them at most department stores or home decorating stores.
- On the day of the meeting, place one of the stars in a zippered bank bag (or some other place where you can protect it from any light), and keep it there until you are ready to use it.
- Place another star in direct light the whole day long. Before the kids arrive, stick that star to the podium or wall of the meeting room.

At the meeting:
Give your prepared message and then ask someone to turn out the lights to reveal the glow-in-the-dark star which had been exposed to the light all day. While the youth look at the glowing star, open up the bank bag and take out the star which was in darkness all day. Tell the group you are placing that star near the glowing star. Chances are no one can even see it in the dark room.

Now ask someone to turn the lights back on. Your youth will be amazed to see two identical stars, side by side. One had spent time in the light and therefore made a noticeable difference in the darkness. The other star had spent the day in the dark bag and could make no difference at all in the darkness of the room.

Jesus urged his followers to "let your light shine before men, that they may see your good deeds and praise your Father in heaven" (Matthew 5:16). If you will spend time each day next to the light (Jesus), you will be able to make a difference in the world.

The Tomato Frog

Deep in the Costa Rican jungle lives the small tomato frog. Red in color like a tomato, he has a unique defense against predators. Once he's attacked, he emits a deadly, milky white poison all over his skin. As the attacking animal bites into a tomato frog, it tastes the poison and spits the frog out of its mouth.

Unfortunately, by the time the predator spits out the frog, the traumatized amphibian dies anyway.

Where to take it from here...

Without question, the tomato frog's poison is effective. The only problem is—it's too late. It's utterly useless in protecting the tomato frog because it's activated after an attack and after the damage is done.

Believers in Jesus often suffer from the tomato frog's bane. We wait to pray and employ our spiritual defenses or offenses until after Satan has already attacked and caused damage in our lives. Only after making a bad decision, breaking a significant relationship, or committing a sin with long-term consequences do we call on the Lord for help. Of course, God can help us in times of trouble. Yet we do ourselves a favor to be in constant prayer and devotion so that the enemy is repelled before the damage is done.

1809

Had you picked up a daily newspaper in 1809, you would have read the big news that Napoleon I, emperor of France, had conquered Austria at Wagram, annexed the Illyrian Provinces (now part of Slovenia, Croatia, Bosnia and Herzegovina, and the Federal Republic of Yugoslavia), and abolished the Papal States.

But in that same year, in France...
- Louis Braille, who devised a way for the blind to read, was born.

And in Germany...
- Felix Mendelssohn, the great composer of symphonies, was born.

And in England...
- William Gladstone, the four-time prime minister and the father of public education, was born.
- Alfred Lord Tennyson, the poet laureate of Great Britain, was born.
- Charles Darwin, the most influential scientist of the nineteenth century was born.

And in America...
- Edgar Allen Poe, the master poet and storyteller, was born.
- Oliver Wendell Holmes, the writer and physician who developed surgical techniques still in use today, was born.
- Abraham Lincoln, the sixteenth President of the United States, was born.

(continued)

But at the end of the year 1809, the only event anyone thought to be important was Napoleon's conquest of Austria. That was the big news.

Today, who remembers the "big news" of 1809? Hardly anyone. Napoleon's conquest is just a tiny blip on the big screen of history. But the world was changed forever by a few seemingly insignificant births that took place that same year.

Where to take it from here...

The year Jesus was born, most people missed it. Only a few were aware of the cosmic implications of his presence in a manger in Bethlehem.

And so it is with all of God's work. Most of it is behind the scenes—hardly ever visible. It rarely make headlines; instead it makes a huge difference in the lives of people because it is eternal.

160

The Good Samaritan Revisited

One day, a priest was walking down a country lane when he heard cries coming from a ditch on the other side of the road.

"Help me! Help me, please!"

The priest stopped and strained his neck to see into the ditch. Then he called across the road, "What happened to you?"

"I was traveling to town when I was attacked, beaten, and robbed. Please help me, I can't move," the voice responded.

The priest paused for a moment. Then he yelled back to the voice in the ditch. "Listen, there's this guy called the Good Samaritan who always helps people in need. He should be coming down the road any time now. He'll help you. I don't know anything about first aid and I wouldn't want to make things worse."

"Wait, you don't understand, I'm..."

But the priest had already gone on his way.

Soon, another man came walking along the road. This man was a Levite.

"Help me! Help me, please!"

The Levite stopped in the road and looked from side to side. "Who was that? Who said that?"

"I did, over here!" called the voice from the ditch on the other side of the road.

"You talkin' to me?" asked the Levite.

"Yes, you! I was traveling to town when I was attacked, beaten, and robbed. I need your help!"

"Oh," said the Levite, gazing into the ditch. "You do sound like someone who could use some help. Wait a minute! Attacked? Beaten? Robbed? What a coincidence. That reminds me of a story a fellow named Jesus told! Ever heard of him?"

"Yeah, I know the story. Now, can you help me?"

(continued)

"Actually, I'm in quite a rush. But I'm sure that someone else will be along shortly to help you. Someone called...um...the Good Samaritan! That's it! He'll be along soon. This is a busy road, you know."

"Couldn't you help me? I'm feeling very weak, I can't..."

"I'm sorry, but I'm not the Good Samaritan. I'm the Levite. If I helped you, it would ruin the story. You wouldn't want me to do that, now, would you?"

"No, I wouldn't want you to do that, but I think it's already...Wait! Come back!"

"Patience there, chap! I'm sure the Good Samaritan will be along shortly," the Levite said as he went on his way.

"Ohhhh...I can't last much longer," the wounded man said softly.

Soon another man came walking along the same road. He ran over to the ditch when he heard the man crying.

"Oh my goodness! What happened?"

"I was traveling to town when I was attacked, beaten, and robbed. Two other men have walked by and haven't helped me. Please help me. I can't move."

The traveler peered in at the wounded figure lying on the ground in front of him. Finally he said, "Wait a minute...you look familiar. Where are you from?"

"Samaria."

"Do you by any chance have a nickname?" he asked, suddenly excited.

"Me? Oh, some people call me the Good Samaritan because I helped an injured man on this road a while back."

"Yes! Yes! Well, sir, I was the man you helped! All this time I have been looking for you because I wanted to pay you back! Wow, this is great! I can't wait until I find my friends and tell them that I actually met up with you again! And now I can finally pay you back! Look, here are two silver coins—exactly what you gave that innkeeper. I feel so much better having finally repaid you. This is wonderful!"

The grateful man, who had himself once been attacked, beaten, and robbed, laid the two silver coins in the dust next to the wounded man and then cheerfully went on his way, whistling a happy tune.

"Wait, wait! I don't want your money..." whispered the man from Samaria. But it was too late. The other man was already gone.

And so, the Good Samaritan died quietly in a ditch by the side of the road.

Where to take it from here...

Jesus told the original story of the Good Samaritan to teach us how to love. But like the grateful man in this take on the parable, we sometimes miss the point. Love is more than words; it's more than a feeling; more than doing what's easy and convenient. Love means getting down in the ditch with someone to give them what they really need. It means getting dirty and being inconvenienced. Sometimes it means laying down your life for a friend (John 15:13). Jesus did that for us.

FAMOUS BUMPER SNICKERS

- Your kid may be an honors student, but you're still an idiot.
- Cover me. I'm changing lanes.
- I brake for no apparent reason.
- Learn from your parents' mistakes—use birth control.
- Forget about World Peace. Visualize using your turn signal.
- We have enough youth; how about a Fountain of Smart?
- He who laughs last, thinks slowest.
- Lottery: A tax on people who are bad at math.
- Change is inevitable, except from a vending machine.
- Time is what keeps everything from happening at once.
- I love cats...they taste just like chicken.
- Forget the Joneses; I keep up with the Simpsons.
- The more people I meet, the more I like my dog.
- Sometimes I wake up grumpy; other times I let him sleep.
- Work is for people who don't know how to fish.
- I didn't fight my way to the top of the food chain to be a vegetarian.
- Where there's a will, I want to be in it.
- Okay, who stopped payment on my reality check?
- Hard work pays off in the future. But laziness pays off right now.
- It's lonely at the top, but you eat better.
- We are born naked, wet, and hungry. Then things get worse.
- Always remember you're unique, just like everyone else.
- Very funny Scotty, now beam down my clothes.
- Be nice to your kids. They'll choose your nursing home.
- There are 3 kinds of people: those who can count & those who can't.
- Why is "abbreviation" such a long word?
- Ever stop to think and forget to start again?

164 ————————————

Some bumper stickers are funny, some are informative, some make you think, others make you mad. In any case they're usually a reflection of the person who is driving the car. If a bumper sticker is funny, you think to yourself, "The person driving this car must have a sense of humor." If the bumper sticker is vulgar and mean-spirited, you might think, "I certainly don't want to meet up with that guy." (Ask the students to react to some of the bumper stickers on this list. What kind of person do you think would have this particular sticker on his or her car?)

When it comes to bumper stickers, the words on the outside of a car are often an indicator of what's on the inside of the car. In the same way, the words that come out of our mouths are often an indicator of what kind of person we are on the inside (James 3:12).

The Test

John Blanchard stood up from the bench, straightened his army uniform, and studied the crowd of people making their way through Grand Central Station. He looked for the girl whose heart he knew, but whose face he didn't—the girl with the rose.

His interest in her had begun when he visited a secondhand book store and selected a book that interested him. When he began to browse the book, however, it was not the words of the book that intrigued him, but the notes penciled in the margin. The soft handwriting reflected a thoughtful soul and insightful mind. In the front of the book he discovered the previous owner's name, Miss Hollis Maynell. It didn't take long to locate her address—she lived right there in New York City. He wrote her a letter introducing himself and inviting her to correspond. The next day he was shipped overseas for service in World War II.

During the next year the two of them grew to know each other through the mail. Each letter was a seed falling on a fertile heart. A romance was budding. Blanchard requested a photograph, but she refused. She felt that if he really cared about her, it wouldn't matter what she looked like.

When the day finally came for him to return from Europe, they scheduled their first meeting—7:00 p.m. at the Grand Central Station in New York. "You'll recognize me," she wrote, "by the red rose I'll be wearing on my lapel."

So at 7:00 he was in the station looking for a girl whose heart he loved, but whose face he'd never seen. I'll let Mr. Blanchard tell you what happened:

"A young woman was coming toward me, her figure long and slim. Her blonde hair lay back in curls from her delicate ears; her eyes were blue as flowers. Her lips and chin had a gentle firmness, and in her pale green suit she was like springtime come alive. I started toward her, entirely forgetting to notice that she was not wearing a rose. As I moved, a small, provocative smile curved her lips. 'Going my way, soldier?' she murmured.

"Almost uncontrollably I made one step closer to her, and then I saw Hollis Maynell. She was standing almost directly behind the girl. A woman

well past 40, she had graying hair tucked under a worn hat. She was more than plump, her thick-ankled feet thrust into low-heeled shoes. The girl in the green suit was walking quickly away. I felt as though I was split in two, so keen was my desire to follow her, and yet so deep was my longing for

the woman whose spirit had truly compan- ioned me and upheld my own. And there she stood. Her pale, plump face was gentle and sensible; her gray eyes had a warm and kindly twinkle.

"I did not hesitate. My fingers gripped the small, worn, blue leather copy of the book that was to identify me to her. This would not be love, but it would be something precious, something perhaps even better than love, a friendship for which I had been and must ever be grateful. I squared my shoulders and saluted and held out the book to the woman, even though while I spoke I felt choked by the bitterness of my disappointment.

"'I'm Lieutenant John Blanchard, and you must be Miss Maynell. I am so glad you could meet me; may I take you to dinner?'

"The woman's face broadened into a tolerant smile. 'I don't know what this is about, son,' she answered, 'but the young lady in the green suit who just went by, she begged me to wear this rose on my coat. And she said if you were to ask me out to dinner, I should tell you that she is waiting for you in the big restaurant across the street. She said it was some kind of test!'"

Where to take it from here...

A test is sometimes the only way we can know what's in our hearts. Knowing we'd need help following him, Jesus taught how we can test our love for him. He said to his followers, "Whatever you did for one of the least of these brothers of mine, you did for me" (Matthew 25:40). Do you really love Jesus? You can find out by noticing how you treat those for whom he died—the poor, the outcast, the sick. When we love them, we demonstrate that we truly love God.

The Stunt Man

In an interview, actor Kevin Bacon shared a conversation he had with his six-year-old son after he had seen the movie *Footloose* for the first time.

The boy said, "Dad, that was really cool how you jumped up on the roof and swung from the rafters. How did you do that?"

"Well, son, I didn't actually do that part," said Bacon. "A stunt man did."

"What's a stunt man?" asked his son.

"That's someone who dresses like me and does things I can't do. Things that are too dangerous."

"Oh. Well, what about that part in the movie where you spin around on that gym bar and land on your feet," persisted the boy. "How did you do that?"

"Well, son, that was the stunt man again, not me. He's really good at gymnastics."

"Oh." A long pause. "Dad, just what DID you do in the movie?"

Bacon sheepishly replied, "I got all the glory."

Where to take it from here...

Jesus stood in for us so that we could have eternal life and share in God's glory. He was nailed to the cross in our place, to pay for our sins, because he was the only one who could do it and emerge victorious.

Too Honest

A police officer stepped up to the driver's window of the speeding car he had just pulled over.

"What's the problem officer?" asked the driver.

"You were going at least 75 in a 55 zone," said the officer.

"No, sir. I was going 65."

"Oh, Harry. You were doing 80 miles an hour," said the man's wife in the seat next to him. The man gave her a dirty look.

"I'm also going to have to give you a ticket for your broken tail light," said the officer.

"Broken tail light? I didn't know I had a broken tail light!" exclaimed the man.

"Oh Harry, you've known about that tail light for weeks," said the wife, who got another dirty look from her husband.

"I'm also going to give you a citation for not wearing your seat belt," said the officer.

"Oh, but I just took it off when you were walking up to the car," protested the man.

"Harry, you *never* wear your seat belt!" said the wife.

Exasperated, the man turned to his wife and yelled, "Shut your danged mouth or I'll shut it for you!!"

The police officer turned to the woman and asked, "Ma'am, does your husband talk to you this way all the time?"

"No, sir," she said. "Only when he's drunk."

Where to take it from here...

Lying has become almost acceptable in today's world. Perhaps we would all be a little more truthful if we had someone like the wife in this story to give us a reality check from time to time.

THE LESSON

Then Jesus took his disciples up the mountain and gathering them around him, he taught them saying:

"Blessed are the poor in spirit, for theirs is the kingdom of heaven. Blessed are they that mourn, for they shall be comforted. Blessed are the meek, for they shall inherit the earth. Blessed are they which hunger and thirst after righteousness, for they shall be filled. Blessed are the merciful, for they shall obtain mercy. Blessed are the pure in heart, for they shall see God. Blessed are the peacemakers, for they shall be called the children of God. Blessed are they which suffer, for theirs is the kingdom of heaven."

Then Simon Peter said, "Do we have to write this down?"

And Andrew said, "Are we going to have a test on this?"

Philip mumbled, "I don't have any paper."

Bartholomew asked, "Do we have to turn this in?"

John whined, "The other disciples didn't have to learn this."

And Matthew asked, "Can I go to the bathroom?"

Judas complained, "What does this have to do with anything?"

And James said, "I don't get it."

Then one of the Pharisees who was present asked to see Jesus' lesson plan and inquired of him, "Where are your theological imperatives and long-term objectives in the cognitive domain?"

And Jesus wept.

Where to take it from here...

Sound familiar? Thankfully the disciples who heard Jesus preach the Sermon on the Mount were good listeners. Unlike some of us, they got Jesus' point. They not only listened well, but they took his message seriously and acted on it.

Do you listen well to God? Do you spend time in his Word? Do you let his instruction change the way you live every day? That's what it means to be a disciple, a follower of Jesus Christ.

Better Not Drop That Egg

"The Easter story is nothing but a myth," Jimmy's high school science teacher announced to his class a few days before Easter break. "Jesus not only didn't rise from the grave," he continued, "but there's no God in heaven who would allow his son to be crucified in the first place."

"Sir, I believe in God," Jimmy protested. "And I believe in the resurrection!"

"Jimmy, you can believe what you wish to, of course," the teacher replied. "However, the real world excludes the possibility of miraculous events such as the resurrection. The resurrection is a scientific impossibility. No one who believes in miracles can also respect science."

"God isn't limited by science," Jimmy responded. "He created science!"

Engaged by Jimmy's outspoken faith, the teacher proposed a scientific experiment. Reaching into his refrigerator, he produced a raw egg and held it up. "I'm going to drop this egg on the floor," he stated. "Gravity will pull it toward the floor with such force that the egg will most certainly break." Fixing Jimmy with a look of challenge, he concluded his proposal. "Now Jimmy, I want you to pray a prayer right now and ask your God to keep this egg from breaking when it hits the floor. If he can do that, then you'll have proven your point, and I'll have to admit that there's a God."

After pondering the challenge for a moment, Jimmy slowly stood to pray. "Dear Heavenly Father," he began. "I pray that when my teacher drops the egg...*it will break into a hundred pieces!* And also, Lord, I pray that when the egg *does* break, *my teacher will have a heart attack and die!* Amen."

After a unison gasp, the stunned class sat in silent expectation.

For a moment the teacher did nothing. At last he looked at Jimmy and then at the egg. Without a word he carefully put the egg back in the refrigerator. "Class dismissed," the teacher said and sat down to clear his desk.

(continued)

The teacher apparently believed in God more than he thought he did. Many people, like that teacher, deny that God exists, yet they run from him, question him, and attack him whenever they get the chance. Jimmy knew God wouldn't strike his teacher dead, but he also knew that his teacher wouldn't bet his life on it.

As the old saying goes, "There are no atheists in foxholes." When your life is on the line, the idea of God suddenly makes a lot more sense.

Not Again!

Two young guys joined a construction crew commissioned to build a multistory office building. At lunch they sat themselves on an iron girder high above the ground and opened their lunch boxes.

"I can't believe it," groaned Joe. "Peanut butter and jelly sandwiches. I don't like peanut butter and jelly!"

With that, he crumpled his sandwiches and hurled them to the ground. Lunch on the second day was a repeat of the first—Joe became visibly upset with the sandwiches in his lunch. Once again, he hurled the sandwiches 17 stories below.

Joe's buddy dreaded lunch on the following day. Sure enough, rather than enjoying a well-deserved rest, he was stuck listening to his new coworker complain. Day after day he silently watched Joe sort through his lunch, exclaim over the offending sandwiches, and send them hurtling to the ground.

"I've had it with peanut butter and jelly!" screamed Joe once again. Angrily smashing the sandwiches in his hand, he thrust them to the ground below.

Unable to restrain himself any longer, Joe's buddy blurted out, "Look, if you don't like peanut butter and jelly sandwiches, then tell your wife not to make them anymore."

"Hey, buddy, wait a minute," snapped Joe. "Don't bring my wife into this. I make my own sandwiches!"

Where to take it from here...

Sometimes we complain about the way things are when we have nobody to blame but ourselves. We are not mere victims of circumstance. We have the power to control what happens to us. But we need to do more than complain; we need to take action.

Trapper John

Living in a remote forest at the northern edge of Canada, Trapper John made his closest friendship with his faithful German shepherd, Duke. Every few days he and Duke would take the overnight trek to check the traps. Selling animal pelts at the trading post in the distant town sustained their simple life.

Trapper John and Duke had shared each other's company for over 10 years, since he had traded a couple of furs for the puppy. The dog loved the man, often protecting him from wild animals when they were out on their all-night treks to check the traps. Duke even seemed to listen attentively to Trapper John share his feelings as he sat by the campfire. Although it was a lonely existence, Trapper John had chosen it.

On one trip into town to sell his furs and purchase more goods, he met her. New in town, this young woman immediately caught his attention. She worked at the trading post and seemed anxious to engage him in conversation. They enjoyed dinner together, and after that John started making more frequent trips into town. That spring they married, and she moved her things out to the trapper's cabin in the woods.

Their first child was born the following winter—but tragedy accompanied the birth of their beautiful daughter, for Trapper John's wife died in childbirth. Broken-hearted, he had no choice but to take his baby girl into town to live with a kind family willing to take care of her until she was old enough to return to the cabin.

She was almost a year old when Trapper John brought her back to his cabin in the woods. Now he was faced with the challenge of raising a child while sustaining their existence with trapping. During his overnight trips, he would leave Duke with the sleeping baby, knowing that he would protect her if she was in any danger. On one such trip tragedy once again visited this small family.

Returning home early in the morning after checking his traps, John came to the top of the hill overlooking his cabin. His heart pounded wildly when he noticed the front door of the cabin pushed open. Throwing down his pelts, he raced to the open door to check on his daughter.

As he entered the cabin, his worst fears were realized. The baby's little bed was covered with blood. In that moment he caught sight of Duke cowering in the corner, covered with blood. Enraged, the man cocked his rifle and pointed it directly at Duke.

"You killed my baby! You killed my baby!" John's anguished roar awoke the baby, who started out of sleep with a little cry from underneath the bloodied blanket. John, his finger on the trigger and his dog in the gunsight, turned his head toward that cry—and with a sweep of his hand, uncovered his unharmed baby. It was only then that he saw the dead bobcat behind his daughter's bed. In a heartbreaking moment of understanding, he realized that he had almost killed the one who had saved his baby's life.

Where to take it from here...

If Trapper John had taken time to get all the facts, he could have avoided this near tragedy. How many times are we guilty of the same thing? We jump to conclusions about other people and judge them before we know the whole story. We sometimes hurt each other because we haven't taken time to get all the facts. In most cases, our understanding of another person's situation is only fragmentary. We need to stop, look, listen, and think before we act.

When Jesus died on the cross, he prayed, "Father, forgive them, for they do not know what they are doing" (Luke 23:34). It was ignorance that nailed Jesus to the cross. Don't make the same mistake today. Don't crucify Jesus all over again by turning your back on him. He is your Savior and friend.

THE TREASURES OF THE CHURCH

The early church had a stormy relationship with the wicked and powerful Roman government. Cycles of severe persecution interrupted by tenuous peace recurred at the whim of the emperor. Roman officials, ignorant of the actual teachings and practices of true Christians, often acted out of bigotry, fear, superstition, or misinformation. The royal court assumed that the growing Christian church operated along the same lines as their own greedy religions.

The emperor, coveting the wealth these Christians must surely possess, summoned their head bishop to the royal court and ordered him to produce "the treasures of the church." The frustrated bishop protested that the church had no gold, jewels, or other valuables (which was indeed true at this point in history). The emperor, brushing aside the bishop's objection, demanded that the riches of the church be brought to him in the morning. The bishop left the royal presence quietly.

The next day the bishop dutifully appeared at the palace doorway. He was empty-handed. "I told you to bring me the treasures of the church!" the emperor raged.

The bishop then invited the emperor to look out at the palace steps. Gathered together, peering sheepishly at the great doors of the royal palace rising above them, was a mass of ragged beggars, cripples, slaves, and outcasts.

"These," said the bishop with a sweep of his arm, "are the treasures of the church."

For his unappreciated but accurate insight, the good bishop was promptly martyred.

Where to take it from here...

You are the treasure of the church. The church is not a building; it is not a doctrine; it is not a program. You are the church, the body of Christ (1 Corinthians 12).

A Bucket of Money

One fine evening a man walked into a fast-food chicken place and bought a nine-piece bucket of chicken. He took his chicken to the park for a romantic picnic under the moonlight with his woman.

Upon reaching into the bucket, however, he received a surprise. Instead of chicken he discovered what was apparently the restaurant's night deposit—nine thousand dollars. The young man brought the bucket back to the store and asked for his chicken in exchange for the money. The manager, in awe of the young man's honesty, asked for his name and told him he wanted to call the newspaper and the local news station to do a story on him. He would become a local hero, an example of honesty and morality that would inspire others!

The hungry man shrugged it off. "My date's waiting. I just want my chicken."

The manager's renewed amazement over the young man's humility almost overwhelmed him. He begged to be allowed to tell the story on the news. At this the honest man became angry with the manager and demanded his chicken.

"I don't get it," the manager responded. "You are an honest man in a dishonest world! This is a perfect opportunity to show the world that there are honest people still willing to take a stand for what is right. Please, give me your name and also the woman's name. Is that your wife?"

"That's the problem," said the young man. "My wife is at home. The woman in the car is my girlfriend. Now let me have my chicken so I can get out of here."

Where to take it from here...

It's easy to look good to people who don't know you. Many of us do a good deed here and there, go to church, say the right words, and everyone thinks we're something that we're not. But God sees your heart (1 Samuel 16:7). It really doesn't matter how much you do or what other people think of you. What matters is what's on the inside.

The Mirror

Author Robert Fulghum tells this story of one of his professors, a wise man whose name was Alexander Papaderos:

At the last session on the last morning of a two-week seminar on Greek culture, Dr. Papaderos turned and made the ritual gesture: "Are there any questions?"

Quiet quilted the room. These two weeks had generated enough questions for a lifetime, but for now, there was only silence.

"No questions?" Papaderos swept the room with his eyes.

So, I asked.

"Dr. Papaderos, what is the meaning of life?"

The usual laughter followed, and people stirred to go.

Papaderos held up his hand and stilled the room and looked at me for a long time, asking with his eyes if I was serious and seeing from my eyes that I was.

"I will answer your question."

Taking his wallet out of his hip pocket, he fished into a leather billfold and brought out a very small round mirror, about the size of a quarter. And what he said went something like this:

"When I was a small child, during the war, we were very poor and we lived in a remote village. One day, on the road, I found the broken pieces of a mirror. A German motorcycle had been wrecked in that place.

"I tried to find all the pieces and put them together, but it was not possible, so I kept only the largest piece. This one. And by scratching it on a stone, I made it round. I began to play with it as a toy and became fascinated by the fact that I could reflect light into dark places where the sun would never shine—in deep holes and crevices and dark closets. It became a game for me to get light into the most inaccessible places I could find.

"I kept the little mirror, and as I went about my growing up, I would take it out in idle moments and continue the challenge of the game. As I became a man, I grew to understand that this was not just a child's game but a metaphor for what I might do with my life. I came to understand that I am not the light or the source of light. But light—truth, understanding, knowledge—is there, and it will only shine in many dark places if I reflect it.

"I am a fragment of a mirror whose whole design and shape I do not know. Nevertheless, with what I have I can reflect light into the dark places of this world—into the black places in the hearts of men—and change some things in some people. Perhaps others may see and do likewise. This is what I am about. This is the meaning of life."

And then he took his small mirror and, holding it carefully, caught the bright rays of daylight streaming through the window and reflected them onto my face and onto my hands folded on the desk.

Where to take it from here...

Jesus said, "I am the light of the world" (John 9:5), and as his followers, we are to be like that little mirror, reflecting the light of Christ into the dark corners of the world. That is the meaning of the Christian life. "Let your light shine before men, that they may see your good deeds and praise your Father in heaven" (Matthew 5:16).

The Cross Room

A young man at the end of his rope groaned in distress as he prayed. "Lord, I can't go on. My cross is too heavy to bear."

"My son," the Lord replied with compassion, "if you can't bear its weight, come with me to the cross room. There you may exchange *your* cross for any other cross you choose."

Filled with relief, the young man sighed, "Thank you, Lord." Briskly entering the cross room, he mindlessly discarded his own cross and searched for one he'd rather carry. He saw many other crosses, some so large the tops weren't even visible. After winding in and out of the rows of crosses, he spotted a tiny cross leaning against the far wall. "I'd like that one, Lord," he whispered.

And the Lord replied, "My son, that is the cross you brought in."

Where to take it from here...

To put your pain in proper perspective, set your hassles aside for a while and reach out to minister to those less fortunate than you. Assisting others to carry their load of suffering helps you recognize that God has blessed you with a lighter burden than you realize. When you pick your cross up again, it will feel a little lighter.

You're Gonna Die

A sick man went to the doctor's office with his wife. The doctor examined the man and ran some tests while his wife waited in the reception area. When the doctor emerged with a concerned look on his face, the wife became anxious.

"Doctor, will my husband be okay?" she inquired.

"I'm afraid your husband is very ill," the doctor replied. "He has a rare form of anemia, and if it is left untreated, he will most certainly die from it. However, there is a cure."

"A cure?"

"Yes. With rest and proper nutrition, the disease will go into remission and your husband should live for many more years. Here's what I want you to do: Take your husband home and treat him like a king. Fix him three home-cooked meals a day, and wait on him hand and foot. Bring him breakfast in bed. Don't let him do anything that you can do for him. If he needs something, you take care of it. Give him a back rub in the morning and full-body massage every evening. Oh, and one more thing. Because his immune system is weak, you'll need to keep your home spotless at all times. Do you have any questions?"

The wife had none.

"Do you want to break the news to your husband, or shall I?" asked the doctor.

"I will," the wife replied.

She walked into the examination room. The husband, sensing that something was wrong, said, "It's bad, isn't it? What have I got?"

His wife answered with a tear in her eye, "The doctor said you're gonna die."

Where to take it from here...

Some of us are like the wife in this humorous story—we say we love others, but we bow out when it comes to putting that love into action. Jesus loved us by serving us and laying down his life for us. His love in action opens up the way for us to have an abundant life. Do you care about others the way Jesus cares about you? When we turn our backs on those who don't know Christ because we don't want to be inconvenienced, it's like we're saying to them, "Too bad. You're gonna die." True love requires action.

Grandma's Ham

Two young newlyweds were preparing to enjoy their first baked ham dinner in their new apartment. After unwrapping the meat and setting it on the cutting board, the wife chopped off both ends of the ham with a butcher knife, tossing the two small ends in the garbage can.

"Wait a minute," said the mystified husband. "Why did you do that? Why did you just cut off the ends of the ham like that?"

"I don't know. My mother always did," answered the wife. "Maybe it helps bring out the flavor."

Unsatisfied with this answer, the husband called his mother-in-law. "Can you tell me why you cut the two ends off of a ham before you cook it?"

"Well," said the mother, "I'm not really sure why. That's just the way my mother did her ham, and it was always delicious."

As soon as he hung up he called his wife's grandmother. "Grandma, we have an important question for you. Can you tell us why you cut the ends off of a ham before you cook it?"

"Oh my yes, dear," answered Grandma in her quiet, thin voice. "I cut the ends of the ham off so it would fit in my pan."

Where to take it from here...

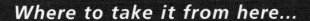

Traditions shape our lives, but it's important to know why we do them. "Because we've always done it that way" doesn't provide enough meaning to keep our traditions from becoming stale and meaningless.

We may have received our worship traditions from great great grandparents, but for us to offer authentic worship we want to understand the meaning behind the traditions. Jesus urged his followers to "worship in spirit and in truth" (John 4:24). If worship seems lifeless and dull to us, perhaps we're just going through the motions instead of being empowered by the Holy Spirit.

Similarly, God welcomes creativity and fresh approaches to serving him. God wants to use you in ways that he has never used anyone before. Let God's Holy Spirit lead you to take risks and try new ways of serving him.

Midnight and the Porcupine

Dave and his family, on vacation in northern Wisconsin, were sleeping soundly when their dog Midnight began whining. It was five o'clock in the morning. Dave got up, stumbled to the door, let the dog out, and then stumbled back to bed. About half an hour later he was awakened again, this time by loud thumping from under the cottage—as though someone was hitting the underside of the floor with a board. Dave pulled on some clothes and went out to investigate.

At first Dave didn't see anything, but then Midnight slowly rounded the house toward him. Bending down to the dog, Dave could make out about a dozen quills sticking out of the dog's fur, mostly on the side of his neck and near the back of his head. Evidently, Midnight had gone after a porcupine under the cottage, gotten nailed with quills from its tail, and the tussle that followed explained the thumping noises on the floor of the cottage.

Stunned, but not in any real pain, Midnight submitted to Dave's handling. But when Dave got the pliers and tried to pull out the quills one at a time, Midnight howled and pulled back. Removing the quills caused excruciating pain, and the dog wanted no part of it.

Dave finally took Midnight to a veterinarian in town, who anesthetized Midnight and then surgically removed the quills. The vet explained to Dave that although Midnight felt no pain from the quills, if they were not removed they would eventually work their way further into his body and head and kill him. Although the surgery was painful, the only way to save Midnight's life was to remove the quills.

Where to take it from here...

Midnight's ordeal illustrates how we often respond to sin in our lives. Like the quills, bad habits and sinful acts become imbedded in our lives. When confronted with sin (by self, a friend, or the Holy Spirit), we tend to recoil. But we must allow God to perform his radical surgery, or those sins will kill us (James 1:13-15).

Contributors

Martin R. Bartel
Sleeping through the Storm

Stan Beard
A Purifying Fire

John D. Brossoit
You Call This a Service Station?

Rick Bundschuh
A Bad Future Investment
The Holy Men
Jenny
No Greater Love
Tossing the Queen
The Treasures of the Church

Tony Campolo
Bad Math, Good Play
The Street Bum

Les Christie
All Is Forgiven
New York Power
A Nobody Named Kimball
The Polish Underground
A Special Special Olympics
Room in the Lifeboats

John Claypool
The Farmer's Three Wishes

Herb Cook
Onion Breath

Ken Davis
Where Did I Come From?

Stephen Deutsch
In the Dark

Ken Elben
The High Dive
A Mickey Mouse Trip

Doug Fields
Donuts at the Back
Monkey Addicts

Greg Griffin
Praise in the Dugout

Stephen James
The Good Samaritan Revisited

Ray Johnston
The Flight of Larry Walters
The Saucer

Andrew Kurkinen
The River

Paul Long
Earthly Treasures

Max Lucado
Come Home

Joel Lusz
The Art Auction
Santa's Trip

Miles McPherson
The Baby Wildebeest
A Bucket of Money
Chip and Dale's Big Push
Get a Bigger Frying Pan
The Tomato Frog

Garland Owensby
Star Light, Star Bright

Kara Eckmann Powell
The Mystery of the Mop
Never Too Late
The Scar Study
Sewing the Sheets

Marci Rice
The Golden Fish

Chris Rush
The Smallest Piece

Joselyn L. San Jose
The Littlest Candle

Kevin Turner
You Call This Justice?

Troy Shaffer
Table for Two

Dave Veerman
The Coach
A Matter of Perspective
Midnight and the Porcupine

Dan Webster
Sammy's Big Catch
Trapper John

Chuck Wysong
The Day of the Rabbit

Jacob Youmans
The Prize

The author and publisher acknowledge that some of the stories in this volume are of unknown origin, having been circulated orally or electronically, and without bylines or other identifying information. We've made every effort to track down the source of every story in this book. We apologize for any omissions.

Professional Resources

Administration, Publicity, & Fundraising (Ideas Library)

Developing Student Leaders

Equipped to Serve: Volunteer Youth Worker Training Course

Help! I'm a Junior High Youth Worker!

Help! I'm a Small-Group Leader!

Help! I'm a Sunday School Teacher!

Help! I'm a Volunteer Youth Worker!

How to Expand Your Youth Ministry

How to Speak to Youth...and Keep Them Awake at the Same Time

Junior High Ministry (Updated & Expanded)

The Ministry of Nurture: A Youth Worker's Guide to Discipling Teenagers

One Kid at a Time: Reaching Youth through Mentoring

Purpose-Driven Youth Ministry

So That's Why I Keep Doing This! 52 Devotional Stories for Youth Workers

A Youth Ministry Crash Course

The Youth Worker's Handbook to Family Ministry

Youth Ministry Programming

Camps, Retreats, Missions, & Service Ideas (Ideas Library)

Compassionate Kids: Practical Ways to Involve Your Students in Mission and Service

Creative Bible Lessons from the Old Testament

Creative Bible Lessons in John: Encounters with Jesus

Creative Bible Lessons in Romans: Faith on Fire!

Creative Bible Lessons on the Life of Christ

Creative Junior High Programs from A to Z, Vol. 1 (A-M)

Creative Junior High Programs from A to Z, Vol. 2 (N-Z)

Creative Meetings, Bible Lessons, & Worship Ideas (Ideas Library)

Crowd Breakers & Mixers (Ideas Library)

Drama, Skits, & Sketches (Ideas Library)

Drama, Skits, & Sketches 2 (Ideas Library)

Dramatic Pauses

Everyday Object Lessons

Facing Your Future: Graduating Youth Group with a Faith That Lasts

Games (Ideas Library)

Games 2 (Ideas Library)

Great Fundraising Ideas for Youth Groups

More Great Fundraising Ideas for Youth Groups

Great Retreats for Youth Groups

Greatest Skits on Earth

Greatest Skits on Earth, Vol. 2

Holiday Ideas (Ideas Library)

Hot Illustrations for Youth Talks

More Hot Illustrations for Youth Talks

Still More Hot Illustrations for Youth Talks

Incredible Questionnaires for Youth Ministry

Junior High Game Nights

More Junior High Game Nights

Kickstarters: 101 Ingenious Intros to Just about Any Bible Lesson

Live the Life! Student Evangelism Training Kit

Memory Makers

Play It! Great Games for Groups

Play It Again! More Great Games for Groups

Special Events (Ideas Library)

Spontaneous Melodramas

Super Sketches for Youth Ministry

Teaching the Bible Creatively

What Would Jesus Do? Youth Leader's Kit

WWJD—The Next Level

Wild Truth Bible Lessons

Wild Truth Bible Lessons 2

Worship Services for Youth Groups

Discussion Starters

Discussion & Lesson Starters (Ideas Library)

Discussion & Lesson Starters 2 (Ideas Library)

Get 'Em Talking

Keep 'Em Talking!

High School TalkSheets

More High School TalkSheets

High School TalkSheets: Psalms and Proverbs

Junior High TalkSheets

More Junior High TalkSheets

Junior High TalkSheets: Psalms and Proverbs

What If...? 450 Thought-Provoking Questions to Get Teenagers Talking, Laughing, and Thinking

Would You Rather...? 465 Provocative Questions to Get Teenagers Talking

Have You Ever...? 450 Intriguing Questions Guaranteed to Get Teenagers Talking

Clip Art

ArtSource: Stark Raving Clip Art (print)

ArtSource CD-ROM: Ultimate Clip Art

Videos

EdgeTV

The Heart of Youth Ministry: A Morning with Mike Yaconelli

Next Time I Fall in Love Video Curriculum

Understanding Your Teenager Video Curriculum

Student Books

Grow For It Journal

Grow For It Journal through the Scriptures

What Would Jesus Do? Spiritual Challenge Journal

WWJD Spiritual Challenge Journal: The Next Level

Wild Truth Journal for Junior Highers